Embracing the Dances of Life

Every Chapter of Life is a Different Dance

John Gasser

WestBow
PRESS
A DIVISION OF THOMAS NELSON

WestBow Press books may be ordered through booksellers or by contacting:

WestBow Press
A Division of Thomas Nelson
1663 Liberty Drive
Bloomington, IN 47403
www.westbowpress.com
1-(866) 928-1240

All Scripture used was attained from Biblegateway.org. NIV Copyright 2010

ISBN: 978-1-4497-1144-3 (sc)
ISBN: 978-1-4497-1143-6 (e)

Library of Congress Control Number: 2011920676

Printed in the United States of America

WestBow Press rev. date: 1/28/2011

I would like to dedicate this book to my beloved
wife Laura Gasser

Contents

Introduction

When you first saw the title of this book, like many others, you probably thought who would write a book on dancing? Isn't that what dance class is for? Perhaps you feel you could learn more about dancing by watching "Dancing with the Stars" on their weekly series. Please understand that is not the type of dancing I am referring to.

Whether you are a professional dancer or whether you have never danced with another person before, everyone has embraced multiple dances throughout life. As is evident by the titles of the chapters, the content throughout this book more accurately addresses the dances we embrace throughout life.

Everyone at one point or another has mountain top experiences and everyone faces life challenges in the valley. Every dance I have experienced throughout life were chapters that convey messages from God that will hopefully help you learn how to maneuver around life's challenges, as well as life's blessings that God sends your way.

Over time I have experienced true intimacy with our Creator like never before. I have felt the Mountaintop experience of God's awesome presence just as Moses did when he was on Holy Ground. Regretfully, I have also fled to Tarshish when God wanted me to go to Nineveh and in doing so, experienced the whale of desperateness while God was allowing me to be chastened. I almost lost everything I had. I am grateful to be restored to the arms of Jesus as I write this book, encouraging all readers to take that leap of faith and embrace the dance with a God who longs to be your most intimate friend.

I know that some readers reading this introduction have a great deal of unanswered questions; questions like "How can a loving God allow innocent people to suffer?" or "How can Jesus truly love all the children of the world and let nearly a third of them starve to death?" I understand by one's self it can be a difficult thing. Be of good cheer. Embrace the dances of life with me through this book. Hopefully the chapters that follow will gain you insight and a clearer understanding as to why God longs to embrace the dance of life with you rather than watching you attempt it alone.

When we learn to embrace the dance with our Creator and Savior, God begins to move mountains in our lives and He begins to restore the years of our youth the locusts have taken away. Consider the nation of Egypt after the seven years of plenty when the seven years of famine began. After the second year of the famine, the Egyptians were hungry and they turned to the government for help. Pharaoh agreed to sell them grain for money. They bought it gladly simply to survive. The following year they had neither money nor grain for food so they gave their possessions to the government for food and they were content. The following year in the seven year drought, they had neither money nor food nor possessions and they gave up their children to the government for grain. They were content for another year. The following year, out of desperation, they sold themselves to become property of the government to endorse a socialistic culture. They were content for another year. By the time the famine was over, everything belonged to the Egyptian Pharaoh and everyone and everything was Pharaoh's possession.

During their times of trial in the seven year famine, that was not the case of the Israelites who had turned to embrace their dance with God. Israel resided in the land of Goshen. God blessed them in a powerful way because they sought divine guidance and provisions from Jehovah. The question we need to ask ourselves today in times of trials; are we going to surrender everything we have to the government expecting hand outs in return, or are we going to the Creator of the universe, who holds the entire universe in the palm of His hand? Louie Giglio said it best in his tour "The Heart of Passion", when he stated "We serve a Ginormous God!" It is my desire that the reading of this book will restore unto you the years of your life the locusts of sin have taken from you so that you can genuinely embrace the dance with God in a powerful way.

To those of you who are the skeptic about spirituality, I applaud your willingness to even pick up this book. I use to be the religious type and in many ways I was religiously wrong in my thinking and understanding. For a season, I embraced the beliefs of my generations prior. I began to see multiple discrepancies with multiple denominational flavors that just did not add up. It wasn't until I took the leap of faith to embrace the dance with God that life for me was truly blessed. Since my embracing the dance with God, I have lived everyday as though it were my last. I have embraced Chip Ingrams "Living on the Edge". Chip will never know the impact he has had on my thought process and my outlook on life. Wow! What a great encounter I've had as I embraced the dance with God. Yet I invite the skeptics of our day. If you just aren't into this God stuff, I understand. If you want to gain insight on the valleys and the mountaintop experiences of life, I dare you to read this writing nonetheless. And hopefully, it will give you perspective you have never had before. So let's get started! God is inviting you to "Embrace the Dance with Him!"

Embracing the Dance with Circumstance

John Maxwell said it best when he stated, "There are some things in life that are placed on us at birth that we cannot change." He continues, "For example, none of us can choose what side of the tracks we're raised on. We can't choose our name, our parents or how we are raised. Nevertheless, beyond being brought into this world the majority of everything we say and do is hinged on personal choice." I use to be the skeptic. I use to embrace the belief that we are all victim to circumstance and there is not a thing we can do about it other than embrace our unfair lot in life. I look back now and realize how ignorant I was. God has removed the blinders from my eyes; I have gained perspective on the Great God we serve and life in general.

Embracing the circumstance

Let me take you back in time. It was July 5th, 1963. As my mother will attest I have been a tenacious fighter since birth. The deck was stacked against me. There were some serious complications in the delivery process that impacted me for 42 years of my life. I am now 47 as I write this book. In the birthing process, God allowed me to embrace the struggle of fighting my way to survival. Like a butterfly embraces the struggle from the cocoon, so I had to embrace the adversity before me. Had He brought me through an easy delivery (if there is such a thing) I never would have embraced the struggle for survival. Finally Doctor Worth empathized with my mother and from old school, clasped my infant skull with fore sips and aligned my head with the birthing canal for delivery. What he didn't know was the fact that he had ushered in permanent brain damage that would go unnoticed until I was four years old. This is not a case for malpractice law suits. Dr. Worth did the best he could and I thank him for it. Little did He know God allowed him to be used as an instrument that would pave the way of my future and to magnify God's Greatness in glory.

Four years later

I remember the night. Every week at our house was quite eventful. I grew up on a dairy farm. It couldn't help but be eventful. Cows to milk, pigs to feed and water. Then you had all of the newborn as well as yearling calves, as they were growing, to be added to the dairy herd. Then you had chickens to feed and eggs to gather. When the cows were milked, the barn floors needed cleaned. Then you had to go feed the cattle and place straw in their stalls to bed down in; especially in the winter months. Don't forget to feed the cats and dogs. They get hungry too. And that is during the slow season when you are neither planting nor harvesting crops from the fields. On top of all that, Dad worked 40 hours a week at Perfect Circle in his spare time. He had a hard work ethic instilled in him in his early years by his dad.

Finally the chores were done. Every Friday night we had our family game night. This was the climactic event of the week I always looked forward to. I lived for game night with the family. That was my currency and I wasn't going to let anything get in my way of game night with family I loved. We were knee deep into the heat of the game called Kaboom. Just as I was a tenacious fighter at birth, I was also a tenacious competitor when it came to games.

Then my currency was invaded by devastation when the next thing I knew, dad and mom were both getting up from the kitchen table to leave the game and the game was not over. I was okay! Why was everyone leaving a game that was unfinished? .... NO!!!!! .... This was my currency! How could it be taken for a crime I did not commit? I had done my chores and I had taken care of my responsibilities in and around the house. Why are you taking what is rightfully mine!!!!!!!! Those were the thoughts racing through my four year old head as I watched them leave. It brought this four year old to tears and I wept like a baby!

What I had not yet grasped was the fact that I had just finished my first recalled seizure resulting from my difficult birth four years earlier. I overheard mom and dad talking in the other room as they reflected over weeks prior, when they recalled me staring into space and not responding to their call. Initially they sloughed it off as a four year old being a four year old. After this devastating night, I will never forget; I embraced this illness as my lot in life. I became the willing martyr. I surrendered to circumstance and remained victim for 41 years of my life. What I failed to realize was the fact that God's hand was on me when I experienced that tragic night and I am convinced that night God wept bitterly as He watched his creation embrace the struggle of circumstance without explanation.

Over time, it did not take a genius to figure out God allowed this tragedy to take place not to become my lot in life, but to demonstrate His glory and majesty as our Creator and Care Giver. God had helped me to embrace the dance of circumstance to gain perspective of His ever-presence in my life. I am grateful for that to this day. God loved me enough to place me in a family who loved me unconditionally, regardless of my own infirmities. God could have placed me with the protective parent that treated me like a porcelain doll in a china cabinet refusing me the right to be broken. I never would have gained the strength and the fortitude I have attained. He could have placed me with parents who would have neglected me because of my infirmities. I never would have been able to receive His love for me through my parents. God could have given me the militaristic parent who would not tolerate imperfection. But instead, God blessed me with graceful parents who overlooked my imperfections and allowed me to be a normal healthy boy in my early years. Mom always said, "When life serves you lemons, squeeze them into lemonade, because lemonade will quench anyone's thirst on a hot day." And I have embraced the dance with circumstance ever since. Thanks Mom and Dad. I'd have never made it without you.

By now there are some readers who are still the skeptic. That's fine. I encourage you to embrace the struggle with reason and faith. Many of you may be thinking that we are all victim to circumstance; that there is no way we can alter it. I agree in part. But if there is a God, a Supreme being if you will, why does He allow adversity to be an active part of the lives we live? Perhaps the following illustration will gain you perspective.

There was a little four year old girl in Kentucky who spent many hours with her maternal grandma while her mom and dad were away at work to make a descent living. Her grandma spent many hours every day working with needle and thread embroidering some of the most beautiful embroidery of her day. One day as she was embroidering, she had the artwork upside down and all the little girl could see was stitches scattered everywhere throughout the quilt and there was no beauty, no pattern and no attraction to the underside of the embroidery she was working on. Finally, one day, the curiosity peaked and the four year old granddaughter approached her grandma and asked, "Grandma, why are you scattering stitches all over the bottom of the embroidery?"

With dimples, the grandma smiled as she embraced the questions of her curious granddaughter. She responded, "Well sweetheart that's easy. Right now you can only see the bottom side of the masterpiece of my art work. You will have a clearer understanding when I am done and turn over the embroidery to show you the masterpiece on the other side. You currently cannot see the masterpiece because I am strategically embroidering it together piece by piece from the underside. When I am finished I will turn it over to show you my masterpiece."

There may be parts about religion, God and the Bible you have never been able to understand the discrepancies. Again, embrace the struggle in your efforts toward enlightenment. I hope and pray as you read on, that the Universe Maker will truly enlighten you to truth and reality as it genuinely is.

1. Going around the room, think of the time when you faced trials that were painful at best that tempered your character? Did you embrace it nonetheless? Why or why not?

2. How did God grace you throughout the trials you have personally encountered? Did it strengthen your faith in God or did you become angry with God? Explain.

3. Why does God allow adversity to be an active part of the lives we live?

4. Read James 1:2-8. What advantage is there to trials? Why should we embrace them?

5. If metal refused to go through the fire, it would never be tempered. It would never obtain its tempered strength potential. When we encounter trials in life, how does it help you to obtain potential you thought previously you never had?

6. Consider the phrase "No Pain, No Gain!" Most athletes will tell you it takes a daily discipline with pain to become the buffed athlete. They keep their sights on what they want to become rather than what they are currently are. What does God want you to keep your sights on when circumstance thrusts fiery trials in your life?

7. Jesus grasped a clear understanding of circumstance when he fasted for forty days and he was hungry. Yet he kept his focus on what his heavenly Father had called him to do, regardless of his limited abilities, while he was in human form. Have we allowed circumstance to cloud our true understanding what God has called all of us to do? If so, explain.

8. Many are confused about our loving Heavenly Father. Many ask, "How can a true loving God let bad things happen to good people?" And yet he has asked us to be like Christ who was obedient to death because He loved us. Talk about a paradox. Could it be, God allows us to be tempered with trials to strengthen and prepare us for the next spiritual battle we encounter? How do you think God disciplines his children in love with circumstance?

9. God redeemed Jesus from the pits of hell three days after he was killed. How has God redeemed you following the trials of circumstance in your life?

10. If we had a time machine that could take you back in time, what period of your life would you go back to change? What part of your life are you less pleased with? Why?

11. Have you surrendered it to the grace of God? Or have you allowed the adversary to guilt you with it even to the point of victimizing you, rendering you powerless? Perhaps, ... Perhaps it's time for you to embrace the dance of circumstance with God, who has your best interest in mind.

Embracing the Dance of Childhood

In every dance I have experienced throughout life, there were chapters that convey messages from God. Hopefully my experiences will help you learn how to maneuver around all of life's challenges as well as life's blessings that God sends your way.

Many reading this book have had some bad childhood memories. I have worked with men who have told me about their childhood memories that were painful to say the least. To be fair to those who have trusted me enough to share the pains of their past with me, I cannot divulge their names but have been given permission to share their stories with alias names. I am grateful they trusted me enough when they were seeking counsel that they were able to open up enough to share their stories.

Consider the childhood Jim had to embrace. Jim was three years old when his dad kidnapped him and his sister and took them out of state away from their biological mother for eighteen months. It took eighteen months for the cops to finally catch up with them and track them down. For eighteen months, Jim and his sister were locked in their rooms and forced to defecate in the room they were locked in. They were fed two meals a day. Everyday they were paraded out to the living room and forced to watch their biological father participating sexually with multiple women in one setting. They were forced to watch because they were beaten if they turned their heads. When the explicit scene had ended, they were escorted back into their room with the door locked behind them.

For eighteen months, Jim had to be a survivalist and caregiver to his younger sister. There were times when he had to be a human shield for his younger sister when she was being beaten by their drunken father. Jim told me the only time he ever saw his dad partially inebriated was when he was demonstrating the orgies, parading before both children. Aside from that, his dad was a mean drunk.

By the time Jim and his sister were found by the police, both had been severely traumatized. Their health had diminished with time. They were finally returned to their biological mother, but it took decades to recover from the traumatic childhood. Like many, Jim struggled to understand how a loving God could allow innocent children to suffer so.

Then there was Steve's situation. Steve never knew his biological father. His dad skipped town when he heard Steve's mom was pregnant. By the time Steve was two, his mother had met a significant other who moved into their house. He brought along his cousin and mooched off of Steve's mom; the only one that worked. The significant other and his cousin had sold themselves with the idea they would babysit Steve every night while Mom was at work. What Mom failed to realize was every night when Mom left for work, both men would start drinking as early as 5:00 pm. Steve would always go to bed at 8:00 just to escape from the inebriated drunks. Steve said each night at 10:00 both men would come in to molest Steve before they passed out in their own beds. Steve had kept it bottled up for two years because he had been threatened they would kill him if anyone found out.

Steve didn't even have a mother who loved or cared for him. Steve said there were multiple times that she labeled Steve as a "Screw-up". He had been called worse but I will refrain from sharing the graphic names given to Steve by his mother and stepdad. Steve was forced to be a survivalist.

Steve was not allowed to establish relationships. At the age of three, Steve had a brother by his mother and stepdad. Through his developmental stages in life, every time Steve met a friend, either his mother or brother would prohibit or intrusively manipulate the friendships started. Steve said it was 17 years of pure hell on earth. Life was miserable. Steve was convinced there cannot be a loving God if He lets this happen to children. Steve said he even resorted to street drugs simply to mask the pains resulting from his horrific childhood.

By the time Steve turned 21, he had broken away from the chains of emotional bondage he had encountered and endured throughout his childhood. However, Steve still has night terrors that relive those painful events of his childhood. Steve will tell you; those past events haunt him everyday causing him to emotionally and socially shut down to become numb about everything and everyone.

As a counselor, my heart goes out to all of the Jim's and Steve's of our day. Your childhood was snuffed out and you never were allowed to be a kid the way God richly wanted you to be. Before you become too critical toward a loving God, I encourage you to look at the history of our country during and following WW II.

During WW II, we were indeed One Nation under God. Church and prayer were encouraged on a daily basis. Bible was even taught in our schools as a history of religious studies and should have been as it was truly part of our heritage as a country. The United States of America was truly One Nation under God's blessings.

In the late 1950's, we had everything we needed. We had an exploding economy. We were internationally recognized as a super power. Then like empires that have collapsed throughout history, we became cocky and self absorbed. Look what we did! We were the determining super power in WW II. Look at our might in The Korean War! We became a proud and stiff necked nation and we didn't need God anymore.

In the 1960's, we began a downward spiral. God did the same thing with America that He did to the nation of Israel and the people of Jesus' day. Romans 1 says:

> [18]The wrath of God is being revealed from heaven against all the godlessness and wickedness of men who suppress the truth by their wickedness, [19]since what may be known about God is plain to them, because God has made it plain to them. [20]For since the

creation of the world God's invisible qualities—his eternal power and divine nature—have been clearly seen, being understood from what has been made, so that men are without excuse.

[21]For although they knew God, they neither glorified him as God nor gave thanks to him, but their thinking became futile and their foolish hearts were darkened. [22]Although they claimed to be wise, they became fools [23]and exchanged the glory of the immortal God for images made to look like mortal man and birds and animals and reptiles.

[24]Therefore God gave them over in the sinful desires of their hearts to sexual impurity for the degrading of their bodies with one another. [25]They exchanged the truth of God for a lie, and worshiped and served created things rather than the Creator— who is forever praised. Amen.

[26]Because of this, God gave them over to shameful lusts. Even their women exchanged natural relations for unnatural ones. [27]In the same way the men also abandoned natural relations with women and were inflamed with lust for one another. Men committed indecent acts with other men, and received in themselves the due penalty for their perversion.

[28]Furthermore, since they did not think it worthwhile to retain the knowledge of God, he gave them over to a depraved mind, to do what ought not to be done. [29]They have become filled with every kind of wickedness, evil, greed and depravity. They are full of envy, murder, strife, deceit and malice. They are gossips, [30]slanderers, God-haters, insolent, arrogant and boastful; they invent ways of doing evil; they disobey their parents; [31]they are senseless, faithless, heartless, ruthless. [32]Although they know God's righteous decree that those who do such things deserve death, they not only continue to do these very things but also approve of those who practice them.

And what happened culturally? In the 1960's, there were riots in the streets and we turned to LSD just to escape it all. The children of God stood in defiance to their Creator and God turned them over to a depraved mind and then United States stood in defiance to God and His principles. So He gave us up to an abased mind and we became God haters in America. Prayer was removed from the schools. Bibles were burned in the streets. The Ten Commandments were removed from the court houses. Churches became corrupted and splintered in every direction of denominationalism. Is it any wonder why our Jim's and Steve's of society got caught in the crossfire of life? It has been evident throughout the history of time that the sins of our fathers have an impact on the third and fourth generation.

God has always had His remnant that He has called to preach and to prophesy and lead people, broken people, back to the foot of the cross. At this point, I come before God on bended knee as I embrace the same plea Daniel made before God in Daniel 9. Daniel cried out to God:

> [3] So I turned to the Lord God and pleaded with him in prayer and petition, in fasting, and in sackcloth and ashes.
>
> [4] I prayed to the LORD my God and confessed: "O Lord, the great and awesome God, who keeps his covenant of love with all who love him and obey his commands, [5] we have sinned and done wrong. We have been wicked and have rebelled; we have turned away from your commands and laws. [6] We have not listened to your servants the prophets, who spoke in your name to our kings, our princes and our fathers, and to all the people of the land.
>
> [7] "Lord, you are righteous, but this day we are covered with shame—the men of Judah and people of Jerusalem and all Israel, both near and far, in all the countries where you have scattered us because of our unfaithfulness to you. [8] O LORD, we and our kings, our princes and our fathers are covered with shame because we have sinned against you. [9] The Lord our God is merciful and forgiving, even though we have rebelled against him; [10] we have not obeyed the LORD our God or kept the laws he gave us through his servants the prophets. [11] All Israel has transgressed your law and turned away, refusing to obey you. "Therefore the curses and sworn judgments written in the Law of Moses, the servant of God, have been poured out on us, because we have sinned against you. [12] You have fulfilled the words spoken against us and against our rulers by bringing upon us great disaster. Under the whole heaven nothing has ever been done like what has been done to Jerusalem. [13] Just as it is written in the Law of Moses, all this disaster has come upon us, yet we have not sought the favor of the LORD our God by turning from our sins

and giving attention to your truth. ¹⁴ The LORD did not hesitate to bring the disaster upon us, for the LORD our God is righteous in everything he does; yet we have not obeyed him.

¹⁵ "Now, O Lord our God, who brought your people out of Egypt with a mighty hand and who made for yourself a name that endures to this day, we have sinned, we have done wrong. ¹⁶ O Lord, in keeping with all your righteous acts, turn away your anger and your wrath from Jerusalem, your city, your holy hill. Our sins and the iniquities of our fathers have made Jerusalem and your people an object of scorn to all those around us.

¹⁷ "Now, our God, hear the prayers and petitions of your servant. For your sake, O Lord, look with favor on your desolate sanctuary. ¹⁸ Give ear, O God, and hear; open your eyes and see the desolation of the city that bears your Name. We do not make requests of you because we are righteous, but because of your great mercy. ¹⁹ O Lord, listen! O Lord, forgive! O Lord, hear and act! For your sake, O my God, do not delay, because your city and your people bear your Name."

Lord, all of us in America have sinned against you and Your Holy Precepts. We are not worthy to be called your children for we have played the harlot. You tearfully turned us over to Satan as we embraced evil of every kind; from idol worship to every sexual sin under the sun. Women have embraced sexual relations with other women. Men have desired sexual relations with other men. I have witnessed all the sin and profanity Satan has hurled into our spiritually degraded culture. Like Rome, our nation's collapse has resulted from self-implosion and we have become morally bankrupt. We wonder why our children today have no moral conscience anymore. The enemy breeds violence. Cults and Wiccan escalate. Columbine claims the lives of the innocent. The shooting of the innocent in the Amish school in Pennsylvania claimed more innocent blood. The shootings and deaths at Virginia Tech. claimed lives of the innocent. Catastrophes have been hurled down against your people who have left You and embraced their own immoralities in life. Oh God, Please, ……. if there is any possible way to restore Your glory and Your might and Your awesome presence in this fallen and degraded society, I come before you. As Daniel prayed, I, your servant, pray that you will return this nation to the humility it must embrace prior to Your return and restoration of these people who have played the harlot.

Now that I have shown you my understanding of what many of the readers of this book have encountered in life, let me share with you a glimpse of the childhood God really intended for you to have prior to our society playing the harlot against Him. God spared me from the treacherous scene many encountered to preserve me for His purpose, just as He did with His remnants throughout history.

I lived a normal childhood for the most part. God was still working on my dad who had been taught a good work ethic, but had never been given time for God or spirituality of any kind. God sent Morris Ball back to the Milroy Christian Church for a second time because there was still some unfinished business, as Gestalt would say. Morris had a bomb of a hotrod car and he knew my dad was a mechanic who loved to work on cars. He continued to routinely bring out his sports car to be looked at by dad. So much so, that dad had dubbed him to be "The Pesky Preacher". Morris had a way of entering my dad's thinking through the back door when the front door had been reinforced.

Morris continued to persuade my dad to go calling with him. Finally out of desperation to get this Pesky Preacher off of his back, dad embraced the invitation to get Morris to leave him alone. Two months later, dad came home after spending the evening with Morris and others and he embraced my mother and said, "Sweetheart, I just wanted to let you know this Sunday I will be baptized by Morris at the Milroy Christian Church.

Perplexed my mom asked why.

Dad replied, "How can I continue to go into people's homes and tell them about becoming a Christian when I haven't become a Christian myself." Years later, I learned my mother had been surrendering in prayer to God on a daily basis. Praying that God would send the right person at the right time to say the right thing to my dad to open his eyes to the truth of Christ. That day, God heard her prayer and He answered it in a powerful way.

From that week on, dad read from the Bible everyday before school as we shared in prayer around the breakfast table. I thank God daily for preparing me for His purpose with a God fearing father who lived his faith rather than simply going through the motions of religiosity and hollow and empty religion that was manmade. God, I am grateful you gave me two parents who reverently feared you.

I was allowed to experience a wonderful childhood because my parents embraced the love triangle Chip Ingram presented in his study manuals. With his permission I would like to parallel his triangle with the Karpman Triangle.

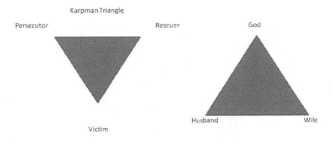

When we embrace God's love triangle, we can share in fellowship with God and our mate. When we defy God the only conflicting triangle we can embrace is the Karpman triangle. There conflict is escalated and it becomes a survival of the fittest. To those whose childhood was taken, I hope the models above will help you to gain perspective. When you were a child, God longed for you to embrace the dance with your childhood years and share with Him daily in fellowship. Regretfully, due to the hard heartedness of your parents, you were caught in the cross fires of life and it really skewed your perspective on the true love of God. Complicate it with the culture's implosion of self destruction, until now many of you have never experienced the dance with your childhood. But be of good cheer. Consider the words found in: 2 Chronicles 7:13-15 (New International Version)

¹³ "When I shut up the heavens so that there is no rain, or command locusts to devour the land or send a plague among my people, ¹⁴ if my people, who are called by my name, will humble themselves and pray and seek my face and turn from their wicked ways, then will I hear from heaven and will forgive their sin and will heal their land. ¹⁵ Now my eyes will be open and my ears attentive to the prayers offered in this place.

Please join with me, humble yourself and pray like you have never prayed before and seek His face. And I guarantee you He will rock your world like never before. Don't just embrace a dead religion at a dead church. No, instead, you need to experience a faith like none other in the arms of Jesus Christ.

1. Knowing this is a very sensitive topic, painful at best for some, I encourage the facilitator to be tender as we discuss this chapter. I encourage the facilitator to start with a story of his dance with childhood. And then incorporate the stories of others in the room. Remember, with topics this sensitive, confidentiality is imperative. Work as a group to encourage one another.

2. Did the stories of Jim and Steve elevate your insecurities experienced when you were a child? Why or why not?

3. Did their stories help you have a clearer understanding of how broken our society has actually been when we no longer had time for God? If so, how?

4. Has this chapter gained you a clearer perspective as to why we have become so broken, apart from the need of a loving God who graciously was the Gentleman who stepped back when we no longer had time for him?

5. How did we allow our culture in America get on a slippery slope with shifting sand? What idols did we worship rather than worshipping and following the God who birthed this great nation? What gods have we been guilty of worshipping in life? What became more important to you than God?

6. If you were blessed with a less than perfect but yet a good childhood, what made you childhood healthy? Were you raised in a church setting? What resulted from the childhood you danced with in your early years?

7. What good memories do you have of your childhood? How did that event impact the character you currently hold?

8. Regarding the relationships you have had to embrace throughout your childhood, which triangle best defines the type of house you grew up in? How did it impact you?

9. Can you recall anyone from your childhood years that was forced to grow up in the midst of the Karpman Triangle that bred chaos and survival of the fittest?

10. Can you recall a child in your youth who encountered the Godly Triangle? Tell about their childhood in contrast to the childhood of the previous question.

11. What stood out to you in 2 Chronicles 7? What can we do to restore what has been taken from us?

12. Do you see a difference between the dead church experiences you have encountered in life and what Jesus actually calls us to? In what ways?

Embracing the Dance with Spirituality

I was blessed to have Christian parents who lived their faith. They did more than talk the talk. They walked the walk and I am grateful for it. Now you have to keep in mind my dad was still a babe in Christ. There were many times he had to maneuver around some of the pitfalls of spirituality. It wasn't long before he started seeing many inconsistencies and discrepancies in Christ's Church. Many times he would witness a high number of Sunday Christians who instead of living their faith would be Christians on Sunday only.

Many Sunday Christians worship their god every Sunday morning in the church buildings. No, that was not a typo. Many who call themselves Christians have reduced the size of the god they worship. They can take their gods out of the box once a week, wipe the dust off, and play church every Sunday morning so it can appease their conscience of guilt. They go through the motions, they fill their pew, they sing their songs without meaning, they put their dollar in the plate, they fidget while the preacher prays, they take communion to see if the juice is spiked, they sleep through the sermon and they are revived back to life when they hear the music playing for the invitation. And all of a sudden, they have been revived with their energy level so they can enjoy the rest of the day doing as they please to enjoy life. That is the kind of god many Christians embrace. It inoculates them but it's not the real thing.

Before I address this further, I need to make a statement, to the skeptics reading this book. What I am about to write is not written to address any matters regarding you nor your participation in worship. I am, however, spending the rest of this chapter to call church leaders to task out of love but embracing the sternness I am about to address. So if you want to see where I step on toes, then read on. Just remember, this is not directed to you personally and so I hope you don't take it as such.

Initially, I was a Sunday Christian. The only reason I went was because mom and dad made me. It was my only way to gain a healthy respect from my dad. I went just like a Sunday Christian. Every week I would remove my little god from the box on the shelf and I would do church just like many others. I called myself a Christian before I was even saved. Everyone else was. It was the cool thing to do. When questioned about my faith, I stammered and stuttered; then would ask mom and dad to answer the question. After they answered I would routinely affirm. "Yeah! That's it!" I was masking the fact that I really didn't know what I believed, much less give it any thought.

Mom and dad would send me to Mahoning Valley Christian Service Camp from the age of eight on. Sometimes I would go a couple times a year. It was great! Why? There were always girls there; good looking girls so I said "Sign me up!" No, I didn't lust after them, nor have evil thoughts about them but they did give me reason to go.

During my third year there, God sent the right person at the right time to say the right thing to get the right response. I was a convicted sinner and I did not know what to do about it. Rod Beheler pulled me aside and walked me through the steps of believing, confession, repenting, and being baptized into Christ for the forgiveness of everything I had ever done wrong. By the end of the week, I was baptized and had taken on a new identity just as my dad had. There were no fireworks or streamers falling out of the sky, but I could tell things had changed.

The god I served was still yet to be defined. I think even through half of my junior year in high school I was still worshipping the god of my parents. I never grasped the fact that God was Ginormous. I had yet to experience my own personal faith. Again, God sent the right person at the right time to accomplish His will in my life. During the Sr. Retreat in September, there was a group their planning to travel on a short term mission trip to build a school building that could additionally be used for worship. The title for the trip was "Haiti in '80". I was fascinated and I had worked on my grandpa's construction crew since I was 12. That was right down my alley.

I went home that weekend to ask my parents if I could go. With much discussion, they concluded that if I could raise my own money for the trip and if I could get the principal's permission, they had no problem with it. I took the first step and went to talk to the principal who stated, you will learn far more in two weeks in Haiti then you could ever learn in a classroom. I didn't quite understand that at the time. Through His faithful and few, God provided the financial means for the trip that would change me for life.

When we arrived at the airport in Porto Prince, the nation's capitol, I experienced culture shock like never before. It was as though God was saying, "John, do you really want to see people living their faith, you haven't seen anything yet?"

To spare you the details, suffice it to say, I was able to embrace a faith in my God rather than the God of my fathers. I learned how big God really is. I committed my life to the cause of Christ that year and I was able to embrace a faith I could live out.

I went to Johnson Bible College, learned how to preach and became an ordained minister of the Gospel. By then I thought I had arrived. Little did I know there were more chapters in my spiritual walk that I had yet to take. My senior year I was preaching in Hot Springs, NC. That took me back 100 years. It was as though I had been warped into a culture that you would have seen back in the 1800's.

Through 12 years of ministry following, I was able to see God's bigger picture and the discrepancies and the dissensions in Christ's church to a point where I am sick of it. I have come to grips with the fact that no church or ministry is perfect, but if we fail to purge the church, we become an apathetic sick church that goes through the motions because they never experience their faith. In part, that has resulted with ministers who have micromanaged the way they do church and they have failed to see how big our God really is. They will make mini gods, idles if you will, that will fit into the way they do church.

I have had a preacher tell me they refuse to invite anyone to preach they do not know. In other words, "No one is worthy of preaching at MY church but ME." To that group I say shame on you. In case you haven't figured it out yet, worshipping God and experiencing your faith in Him is not about me and it's not about you. It's about HIM!!!!! Sometimes God attempts to send the right person at the right time to say the right thing and many ministers of the gospel will block the efforts of God. The battle we fight is not against flesh and blood, but against principalities of this dark world. To preachers who fit this description I say this, "Repent, for God is not well pleased with your sacrifices."

In addition, micromanagement ministers can't let church families grow much greater than 100-150 in size. Any larger than that is more than one man can micromanage. In this setting the preacher has to pick out the worship style. He is the only one qualified to pray, preach, teach, organize and shepherd. No one else is trained to do it all. (It is also the only way he can maintain job security). Many churches have embraced the micromanagement ministers. This way they can let him do all the work while they take down their gods out of the box, wipe off the dust and fill the pew while worshipping their little gods while going through the motions of filling their seat in the sanctuary. Wow! That's the type of ministry I'd sure not want to be a part of. That's too close to idolatry to me. Some worship the god of music. Others worship the prestige of identity with a group; others worship the god of apathy.

The first three of the 10 commandments address our relationship with a righteous and jealous God. If there is one thing I have learned over time, it's the fact that God don't play. You are either in or out of His will. There is no room for lukewarmness.

To the ministers who micromanage ministry for job security, I say repent! The majority of this group struggle to even believe that there is a literal hell that the Bible tells us about. Many are like the church leaders of Jesus' day and He called them white washed tombs. "You appear clean on the outside but on the inside you are full of dead men's bones." In Matthew 7 Jesus warns against false prophets. Jesus said:

> [13]"Enter through the narrow gate. For wide is the gate and broad is the road that leads to destruction, and many enter through it. [14]But **small** is the gate and narrow the road that leads to life, and only a **few** find it.
>
> [15]"**Watch out for false prophets.** They come to you in sheep's clothing, but inwardly **they are ferocious wolves.** [16]**By their fruit** you will recognize them. Do people pick grapes from thorn bushes, or figs from thistles? [17]Likewise every good tree bears good fruit, but a bad tree bears bad fruit. [18]A good tree cannot bear bad fruit, and a bad tree cannot bear good fruit. [19]**Every tree that does not bear good fruit is cut down and thrown into the fire.** [20]Thus, **by their fruit you will recognize them.**
>
> [21]"Not everyone who says to me, 'Lord, Lord,' will enter the kingdom of heaven, but **only he who does the will of my Father who is in heaven**. [22]Many will say to me on that day, 'Lord, Lord, did we not prophesy in your name, and in your name drive out demons and perform many miracles?' [23]Then I will tell them plainly, **'I never knew you. Away from me, you evildoers!'**
>
> [24]"Therefore everyone who hears these words of mine and puts them into practice is like a wise man who built his house on the rock. [25]The rain came down, the streams rose, and the winds blew and beat against that house; yet it did not fall, because it had its foundation on the rock. [26]**But everyone who hears these words of mine and does not put them into practice is like a foolish man who built his house on sand.** [27]**The rain came down, the streams rose, and the winds blew and beat against that house, and it fell with a great crash.**"
>
> [28]When Jesus had finished saying these things, the crowds were amazed at his teaching, [29]because he taught as one who had authority, and not as their teachers of the law.

I have seen many churches who have been ravaged by wolves in sheep's clothing. As a result those church families embraced the dance of spirituality with Satan. That's why spiritual warfare is fierce in any church who practices purity and accountability and true worship of our Great God, Jehovah. Satan loses his grip when the church executes discipline as defined in I Corinthians 5. Knowing I've made some squirm already, you had better put on your seatbelt before you go any further. I hope you will understand I am writing this because like the prophets of old, they had to do the unpopular thing of calling God's people to task, because then and only then would He hear their voices.

In I Corinthians 5, Paul was doing the unpopular thing when he wrote:

> [1]It is actually reported that there is sexual immorality among you, and of a kind that does not occur even among pagans: A man has his father's wife. [2]And you are proud! Shouldn't you rather have been filled with grief and have put out of your fellowship the man who did this? [3]Even though I am not physically present, I am with you in spirit. And I have already passed judgment on the one who did this, just as if I were present. [4]When you are assembled in the name of our Lord Jesus and I am with you in spirit, and the power of our Lord Jesus is present, [5]**hand this man over to Satan, so that the sinful nature**[a] **may be destroyed and his spirit saved on the day of the Lord.**

> [6]Your boasting is not good. Don't you know that a little yeast works through the whole batch of dough? [7]Get rid of the old yeast that you may be a new batch without yeast—as you really are. For Christ, our Passover lamb has been sacrificed. [8]Therefore let us keep the Festival, not with the old yeast, the yeast of malice and wickedness, but with bread without yeast, the bread of sincerity and truth.

> [9]I have written you in my letter not to associate with sexually immoral people— [10]not at all meaning the people of this world who are immoral, or the greedy and swindlers, or idolaters. In that case you would have to leave this world. [11]But now **I am writing you that you must not associate with anyone who calls himself a brother but is sexually immoral or greedy, an idolater or a**

slanderer, a drunkard or a swindler. <u>With such a man do not even eat.</u>

[12]What business is it of mine to judge those outside the church? **Are you not to judge those inside?** [13]God will judge those outside. **"Expel the wicked man from among you."**[b]

When we fail to expel the wicked **<u>who calls themselves brothers</u>**, Satan smells blood and he will strike the four corners of the church and the church built on sand cannot withstand the storms of Satan.

It is time to purge the churches across the land. God has no time for mambee pambee people who call themselves Christians. They make Him sick because the God I serve is a jealous God who will not tolerate such a people. God has called His people to battle in a spiritual warfare and many have yet to even go through boot camp, much less be prepared for battle. Joshua said it best following God's conquering of the land of Canaan.

"If serving the LORD seems undesirable to you, then **choose** for yourselves **this day** whom you will serve, whether the gods your forefathers served beyond the River, or the gods of the Amorites, in whose land you are living. But **as for me and my household, we will serve the LORD."**

1. What are some of the gods you have witnessed people in your church community worship? What routines have become paramount, so much so that it has stifled the ongoing growth God has called us to?

2. Why have so many churches embraced the inoculation of the real thing when it comes to experiencing spirituality?

3. If someone approached you with spiritual questions and was seeking scripture reference, would your response be shallow? Or would you have the meat of the answer? Why?

4. Why are we so critical of the sinners of our culture who have been ravaged by the adversary, when we all are so broken from the sins in our own making?

    - What was Jesus' response to the religious people of his day who were smug against the sinners? John 8:6-8

5. Shouldn't we humble ourselves and soberly assess our own sins we have embraced throughout life? We are called to confess our sins to one another with a repentant heart.

    [15] And the prayer offered in faith will make the sick person well; the Lord will raise them up. If they have sinned, they will be forgiven. [16] **Therefore confess your sins to each other and pray for each other** so that you may be healed. The prayer of a righteous person is powerful and effective. - James 5:15-16

6. Have we become too self-righteous and too self-absorbed to open up to others in confession? What are the advantages of confessing our short comings in life?

7. How do micro-managed ministries limit the effectiveness of the gospel? How far do you have to go in your own community to find church communities who have been blinded from the truths of the full Gospel?

8. Why do the first three of the Ten Commandments center around our relationship with God? Have you ever had anything that you valued more than God? A car? A home? Relationships?

9. Have you ever taken a self-assessment on you spiritual walk with God? What were the results? What areas of your spiritual walk have improved since the birth of your faith?

10. Why do many churches slack in spiritual disciplines God has called us to with those who call themselves brother/sister?

11. How can accountability strengthen the churches? How many are you accountable to? How many have you been genuine with at every level in love?

12. How do you feel the adversary has ravaged your church in times past? How did the leadership manage it and what did they learn in the process?

Embracing the Dance of Marriage

Throughout my educational years, I was always the odd duck out. As I had stated in the first chapter, I was a born epileptic. Epilepsy was never your best friend when it came to sizing up with peer groups. I never had to be popular though. I had accepted it as my lot in life. But in my eyes, I was normal just like everyone else. I am certain many girls eyed me as a good possibility but when sized up against peer popularity, even the thought of going with an epileptic would bring your peer inclusion to a screeching halt. But I was okay with that. I think because I was content with that, I was able to mature more quickly than my peers at school. I was convinced God would send the right girl at the right time for the right purpose of blessing me with a help mate. I had many girlfriends from church or church camp. As my mother will attest there were times I had two on the string at the same time. I wasn't married and I had no problem playing the field. And I loved it.

Then in the summer before my senior year, I went to camp as always. Remember, if there are girls there, sign me up! But that year, my older sister Carol had been bummed by losing her boyfriend. We had always been close and she always leaned on her little brother when she was bummed. I was okay with that. She was my sister. What I overlooked was the fact that many of the girls at camp saw me with Carol a great deal and they assumed we were boyfriend/girlfriend. I love my sister, but she wasn't worth the sacrifice of an

35

entire week God had given me to size up the girls on campus. I interacted with many girls from all across the region. In fact, we had reached a free time on the scheduled events so our entire group I was in decided to take off for the woods where one of the largest red oaks stood. It was often used by teams to go out and get group photo shots for everyone to take home with them to remember one another and even keep in touch via snail mail. Yes, I realize that dates me at this point. Believe it or not, we use to be able to survive without computers and cell phones.

We got back to the tree when I realized there was some who meandered back with us that was not on our team. So we asked if they would be willing to use everyone's cameras to take our team photo. They agreed to do so. So every one of us on the team began to scurry up the mighty oak for the photo shoot; .... And then it happened. God allowed the right thing to happen to the right person at the right time to achieve His purpose. .... Have I got you on the edge of your seat yet? .... As I was climbing up the tree, I was about 20 feet up in the tree when my footing began to slip and I quickly grabbed the nearest branch to stabilize myself and it went SNAP!!!!!! I immediately went hurling out of the tree and a dried up piece of real estate didn't have much mercy on impact. Painful as it was I couldn't help but notice the very attractive young lady's feet whom I had fallen toward. Concerned about my well-being, she asked if I was okay. My proud self wanted to buff up in front of her to show her I was alright, so once I got my breath, I proceeded to stand up as if nothing had happened to me I couldn't handle. But my proud self was immediately diminished when I realized I had thrown my back out and had to leave camp early that year. That was okay, I'd be back for the Sr. Retreat. I wasn't going to let fate lick me just because there was a brief set back.

I went to the chiropractor and he made me as good as new and I returned to work with my grandpa the following Monday. I was one of the few 16 year olds making $15.00 per hour at the time. Remember, I had been working with him since age 12. So I was able to own livestock, a truck, a car and even a Honda 350cc. The only thing I didn't have was a driver's license. You don't need a license to drive on the farm. I was too busy to take driver's education, so I opted to wait until I was old enough to be licensed without the education.

On Wednesday, I walked in the house to set my lunchbox in the kitchen, when Carol, my older sister, squawked out, "You got a phone call from a girl!"

"Who?"

"Her name is Laura Thomas. She said she met you at camp last week."

"What did she want?"

"I don't know. She left her phone number and it's a local number. I told her you would call her when you got home from work."

"I've got chores to do. I'll call her when I come in for the evening."

Laura Thomas? I didn't recall a Laura Thomas. I remembered a great deal of the girls from camp, but I certainly didn't recall a Laura Thomas. I wonder what she wants; my address to be a pen pal? And how did she get my phone number? Then it hit me. I was the 5th consecutive generation of John Gasser's each with different middle names. Yeah you guessed it, she found my dad's number in the phone book. Whatever she wanted it must be important.

I finally came in for the night and returned the call. Laura was a very timid and shy girl. In fact to this day she identifies herself as painfully shy in both school and in every public setting. She was the good girl who refused to lower her standards for popularity. In fact, the ONLY reason she even called me initially was because her older sister Ramona kept pestering her with lines like, "Stop being a chicken! I'd call him if I were you!" She finally succumbed to the inevitable and made the call while I was still at work. When she had hung up from the conversation with Carol, Ramona locked eyes with Laura and said, "I would never have done that in a million years!!!!!!" God had to use Ramona and Carol just to keep me on track with His divine purpose.

As I returned the call, you could hear the nervousness of Laura's voice. I still had no idea who she was. She said her parents were taking their annual trip to Kings Island and each of the girls got to take one friend and she was extending an invitation to me. I didn't even recall what she looked like. I didn't want to go on a date with a mud fence. Talk about dilemma! My thoughts began racing. "Kings Island! .... Risk? .... Kings Island! .... Risk?" Finally, I figured she can't be all that bad if she was at camp. Camp had been good to me in years prior and besides, it was a free trip to the theme park. Count me in!

That weekend at Kings Island God began a new chapter in my life. Laura was everything I had always wanted in a girl. I still struggled in recalling Laura's presence at camp so I asked where and when she first noticed me.

Her reply? "Don't you remember falling out of the tree?"

"Yeah!"

.... "You fell to my feet when you hurled out of the tree."

"Oh Yeah! You were the one holding all the camera's when I fell at your feet." (I don't recommend to any man falling for their woman the way I did. I literally **fell** for her.)

We had a blast at the theme park. But no bells went off that day. It simply started the process. I had yet to see Laura as being any different than the rest of the girls. Remember, I was a player.

The following weekend, I figured I owed her a date to express my appreciation for her inviting me to Kings Island. So I took her to the movies to watch "Black Beauty". We then went to McDonalds for supper. Remember, there were no bells yet. I was still sizing her up. Good looking? Check! Good personality? Check! A Christian? Not yet! Sweet disposition? Check! Low maintenance woman? Check! A team player? Check! Compassionate? Check! Submissive to authority? Check! All along the way, God almost had to beat me over the head with a 2x4 before I realized this woman was authentically real and she was the one God had ordained for me to marry someday.

I really knocked her socks off. That evening I walked her to her front door and graciously turned toward my car after expressing how grateful I was to have met such a beautiful woman. I never laid a hand on her nor even gave her a kiss goodbye. Her immediate response? "What's wrong with this guy?" .... Now, keep in mind this woman was use to encountering guys who had an agenda; guys who had every intent to score a home run prior to the marriage scene. "And this guy didn't even give me a goodnight kiss." Puzzled, she didn't know if this was a good thing or a bad thing.

Throughout the busy weeks, Laura and I kept in contact via phone. It was local so my parents allotted one hour per night as our limit. I was okay with that. I had a busy life style anyway, at least at the time. Long about the seventh week of dating, there came a time of redefining of the relationship. Are we just best friends or did we want to court one another closing the right to date any other. It came to our seventh date night. Being the leader of the relationship, as God has called all of us men to do, we went out on the seventh date. At the end of the date, I asked if Laura wanted to go steady with me. To show you how this was so of God, her response was, "I don't know." I asked what was holding her back. "Well, I have been dating Paul as well. I need time to think about this."

I drove off that night very slowly, assuming I would never see Laura again; at least not on a date. Now I was bummed. I was there for my sister when she was bummed. No one was there to comfort me when I was bummed. Jesus knew what it was like to be bummed and have all of His friends desert him. I know the intensity for me was not as great but I knew I had a Savior who sympathized with me. In fact Jesus experiences the same emotion every time He invites us into His purpose and we say "No! ….. Not right now. I love too many other things and too many other relationships to commit to Your cause right now Jesus. Save it for another day and if I have time, I will make room for You then. Finally that evening as I was lying down to sleep, I surrendered my relationship with Laura to God. "God if she is the one You have chosen for me, please make it known to me somehow." And then I went to sleep.

I didn't even call her for a few days. I gave her time to think about it and time for God to have his way with both her and I. By this time she had concluded the night I asked and the night she wasn't certain who she wanted to go steady with me, she was convinced I'd never come back to her. Compound that with phone calls stopping, in her mind she was beating herself up for fear she had made a grave mistake. "After all, why in the world did I obsess about Paul? He has tried multiple times to hit the homerun date and failed miserably on every corner. John on the other hand didn't even push me to embrace a goodnight kiss. When he finally did, it was simply a peck on the cheek." And God worked diligently on Laura during those 72 crucial hours.

Finally, I was moved to call her mid week. She was very timid and shy, fearing the worst. I asked what was wrong. "After last Saturday, I figured I'd never hear from you again."

"Why is that?"

"Well, when you asked if I'd go steady with you and I said I didn't know, I figured that was it and it was doubtful I would ever hear from you again."

"Why's that?"

"That's just the way it normally works for me when I am dating guys."

"Look, I've told you I love you. That's not conditional. If you need time to think about it, then you need time to think about it. I'll wait until you are ready to decide. The main reason I called tonight was to see when you would be available for another date. No strings attached."

In the back of her mind she was asking, "Is this guy for real?" He's going to accept me on my terms? Her attraction to me became elevated that night. "He really cares about my needs and my comfort level. There's something uniquely different about this guy and I like it!" She accepted the invitation and we continued to date without going steady for a couple more weeks. I believe the willingness to allow her to decide when she would allow the defining of the relationship to occur expedited her decision. Two weeks later, at the end of the date it went like this.

"Do you remember our date night three weeks ago?"

"Yeah!"

"Well, I've given it some thought and if the invitation is still current, then I'd love to."

"Are you all in?"

"Yes, I'm all in!"

"What about Paul? Is that going to be fair to him?"

"He doesn't really love me that much since he has never had his way with me. I looked back and realized the only time he has really wanted me was when he didn't have another woman on the string. No one has genuinely loved me like you have. I love you too!"

We embraced and I went home that night on clouds. I couldn't even sleep! It was so of God to reveal Himself in a relationship He almost had to beat me over the head with the 2x4 because I wasn't staying in His will. This was one of the first of many teachable moments for me. The lessons I learned from this entire relationship are as follows.

1. Never rush into a relationship. If you rush in, you get what you paid for.

2. Secondly, pray and trust God to bring you the right type of mate, where you can complement and complete one another. When you rush into a relationship and play God, God removes Himself and His blessings from you.

3. Go through the biblical process of courtship and understand that a life long relationship has seasons: attraction, dating, courtship, marriage, intimacy and lifelong commitment to one another unconditionally. (Don't make a commitment you don't plan to keep.)

4. When in conflict, (yes, there will be conflict), embrace the biblical model of confession and repentance. It goes a long way in leading to the grace you will both long for.

5. It is imperative that both you and your mate embrace the love triangle with your Creator. Then and only then will God's Blessings unleash on you.

The rest of the relationship in the dating season ran its course. She got to know all about me and I got to know all about her or so it seemed. My dad disagreed though. For months he took a back seat and watched Laura and I embrace the dances of dating and courtship. We were engaged to be married twelve months after our first encounter with one another. Three weeks prior to the marriage, dad took his position of resistance to the marriage. He and I had a heart to heart talk.

"Dad, I love her and we have done the dating proper."

"Yes you have and I am grateful you have but you are not ready."

"Why not?"

"Neither of you have ever engaged in conflict."

"I didn't know we were suppose to. I thought we were suppose to love each other not conflict."

"I suppose you think you and her will never conflict throughout your entire marriage?"

"I don't suppose."

"And that's why you need to conflict prior to the marriage ceremony so you will know how to handle one another in conflict while maneuvering through your married life in harmony, rather than praying for an early death."

There was a great deal of wisdom in Dad's position regarding his wanting the best for my future. He had the same defining moment with my mother prior to their marriage. Mom was raised in a home where anger was displaced by yelling at one another. Dad on the other hand, engaged in conflict in calm voices seeking resolution and restoration to relationships even if you agreed to disagree on certain issues. He made it clear that yelling, screaming, temper tantrums and throwing things was not an option and if she could not submit to that defining of the relationship, the wedding was off. I thank God, for my mother who has submitted to the leadership of my dad. He never lorded over her but he had mastered being firm in love and grace.

I needed the same defining of the relationship between Laura and I. As with most weddings, the closer the wedding date gets, the higher the stressors and tension become elevated. Then it happened. Yes, you guessed it. We engaged in conflict for the first time in our relationship. It was a defining moment of the relationship. I am grateful to have had a beautiful woman willing to submit to my leadership under God's providence.

We sealed the deal on July 5th, 1981 and we have been committed to one another through thick and thin. We have dealt with many challenges in life together. We embraced each of them one at a time and with God's divine intervention, we have travailed through each of them with grace. I feel truly loved by this wonderful woman God had ordained to be my wife. Two words define our marriage; "No regrets!" As the prison system identify life sentence inmates as "Lifers", that's my commitment to the woman I love. I am in it for life! She has won my heart for life.

I have a very hectic work schedule that requires 60-70 hours per week. Needless to say we are apart more than together. To stabilize our marriage, every week we have a date night. Every week, Laura knows she will have my undivided attention 8- 12 hours a week to invest into each other. Sometimes it comes in two increments of 4 hours per event. Having three children really tested our commitment to one another. Each of the kids have tested our commitment to one another and they have all attempted to crash mom and dad's date nights. I am grateful we pulled together as a team and kept the children from invading that crucial time together. Amazingly, each of them has admitted they hope they can find a mate that commits to the cause of strength in their own marriage someday.

Marriage is a life time investment that we need to make on-going love deposits on a routine basis. Like airplanes, you can put relationships on auto pilot for a brief time, but not indefinitely. Marriages are the same way. When needs and demands crowd your space for "us time", they can only withstand a brief auto pilot course before routine maintenance and check ups are imperative. If you stop investing in one another on a routine basis, you will cheat yourself and your marriage out of the dividends you could have had, had you actually treated it as such.

Sweetheart, before all of these readers, I want you to know I am committed to investing into our marriage and in you on a routine basis. I promise this so that we may draw dividends from the investments we've created as we grow old together. I love you, Gorgeous!

1. Starting with the facilitator, go around the room and share your story. What brought you and your mate together? For those not yet married, tell about the relationship that stands out most to you throughout the dating season?

2. What are some of the pitfalls you recall about the dating scene? If you could go back in time, what would you have done differently?

3. In reflection, where was God in the relationship between you and your mate? Was it bathed with prayer? Were you seeking God's will for your relationship? Why or why not?

4. Have there ever been times when you were disappointed by your mate? Did you grace your mate or did you polarize against your mate?

5. When you were sizing up your mate, what criteria in your mate were you looking for? Why? Were you ever tempted to lower the bar of expectation for fear no one would love you otherwise? If so, what resulted?

6. For those married, when you were in the dating season, you were proactive at every level in the dating scene. How did you cultivate ongoing dating after you said "I do"?

7. When in conflict, how often have you graced your mate the same way God graced you? We demonstrate a great deal of grace when we are dating. Why do we stop gracing one another after the marriage?

8. Why do so many rush into relationships? How does that stack against God's design for relationships and marriage?

9. How have you invested into the relationship with your mate? Has it been an ongoing investment with dividends? Why or why not?

10. If you had a phrase that defined your marriage relationship with one another and with God, what phrase or phrases would define your marriage/relationship?

11. How would you like to be wooed by your mate in the ongoing relationship? God woos us every day through the Holy Spirit. How would you like to develop memories of a legacy?

12. To have a rock solid marriage, both of you need to love God first and one another second. Where is God in your love life right now? If it is out of synch, what can you do to put priorities in the right relationships God has called us to?

Embracing the Dance of Parenting

In today's culture, parenting is not for sissies. Parenting is hard work. Our children are bombarded with peer pressures and sexuality at an earlier age every year. The media has flooded our culture with existential thought that license children to embrace the motto, "If it feels good, do it" mentality. Many of our youth possess no moral conscience. I am grateful I didn't have the challenges many parents face every day in the raising of their children.

I have encountered many parents who have limited parenting skills because of the house or houses they grew up in. Many grew up in single parent homes. They are either all nurture with limited discipline or they are disciplined without being nurtured. Families have lost their equilibrium since divorce has ravaged our culture. Children have been beaten, abused, neglected or abandoned. Is it any wonder why they are clueless when it comes to the parenting of the next generation?

Yet if we genuinely want to embrace the dance of parenting as God has called us to do, we can equip the next generation to prepare and maintain equilibrium in the faith based households they have been given.

My parents embraced the dance of parenting with grace; much grace. Attending church was not optional. Anyone who resided at our house understood that. There were even troubled teens my parents brought in under their wing to mentor. Even they knew attending church regularly was not optional. The spiritual training was priority one just as it has been called for us to do since the beginning of time. Jews trained their youth about the deliverances they encountered throughout the Pentateuch and the historical books of the Old Testament. Children were taught about the prophets of old who were God's messengers from Jehovah God Himself. Knowing the history of their faith was crucial to their training before boys celebrated their Barmitzpha.

Our forefathers embraced the same parenting style when they birthed this nation of ours into religious freedom under a limited government. If you go to Washington D.C., it is written all over the buildings and monuments. Consider the first two paragraphs in our Declaration of Independence.

"When, in the course of human events, it becomes necessary for one people to dissolve the political bands which have connected them with another, and to assume among the powers of the earth, the separate and equal station to which the laws of nature and of **nature's God entitle them**, a decent respect to the opinions of mankind requires that they should declare the causes which impel them to the separation."

> **"We hold these truths to be self-evident, that all men are created equal, that they are endowed by their *Creator* with certain unalienable rights that among these are life, liberty and the pursuit of happiness.** That to secure these rights, governments are instituted among men, deriving their just powers from the consent of the governed."

I was raised by parents who embraced the same understanding that it was their responsibility to raise faith-based wholesome children to pass the torch to as they grew older. Procreation was God Ordained. As long as God is actively involved in the parenting of a family, wholesome and genuine Christian children result.

Regretfully, in many homes over the past 50 years parents have not had time for God. Satan has flooded our culture with materialistic lifestyles. This has pulled us away from our Creator and His purpose in parenting the children He has blessed us with. After all, everyone else is doing it. And we have to keep up with the Jones'. We can make time for God when we retire. Right now, I have to pursue this career or this dream or this club or this yacht or this trip. When we get older we can entertain it then. And so we pursue our materialistic dreams without counting the cost. Our marriages are put on hold. Our families are put on hold. Our parental responsibilities are put on hold. Most Christian parents have no clue what Proverbs 22:6 says about parenting. For those who have vacated their relationship with God and have failed to turn to His Word for guidance, Proverbs 22:6 says:

> [6] Train [a] a child in the way he should go, and when he is old he will not turn from it.

Ephesians 5 says:

> [1]Children, obey your parents in the Lord, for this is right. [2]"Honor your father and mother"—which is the first commandment with a promise— [3]"that it may go well with you and that you may enjoy long life on the earth."[a] [4]Fathers, do not exasperate your children; instead, bring them up in the training and instruction of the Lord.

Titus 2 says:

> [6]Similarly, encourage the young men to be self-controlled. [7]In everything set them an example by doing what is good. In your teaching show integrity, seriousness [8]and soundness of speech that cannot be condemned, so that those who oppose you may be ashamed because they have nothing bad to say about us.

As was evident in the second chapter of this book, some children who have been caught in the crossfire of our culture's self indulgences and they haven't a clue about what the manual that God ordained throughout time actually says. It's like assembling a piece of equipment or the swing set for the kids without reading the manual. Yeah you may get it together in a different way then what the manual calls for, but it is not likely it will last as long or will meet its full potential of functionality. Instructions in the parenting manual of the Bible are absolutely imperative to the success of raising a family and parenting Christian children into young adulthood.

Exacerbate that with the inability to discipline children appropriately as defined in the manual and you birth a generation that now has to include unruly children in the Diagnostical and

Statistical Manual –IV edition for Conduct disorder or Oppositional Defiant Disorder. Thanks to Dr. Spock, corporal punishment that served our country well for decades prior, was shunned by media and supposed research that concluded spanking a child impaired their self image and self esteem. Spanking on the derriere was equated with child abuse. Bold Christian authors like Dr. James Dobson cried out against the ludicrous belief that children should never be disciplined with corporal punishment.

With broken homes and unruly children, it wasn't long before an angry generation of children permeated our society. Teachers can't administer discipline at school or they will be fired. Parents can't discipline their children or the children will be reported and removed from your homes. Proverbs 13:24-25 was removed from the principles our country was founded on.

> 24 He who spares the rod hates his son, but he who loves him is careful to discipline him.

> 25 The righteous eat to their hearts' content, but the stomach of the wicked goes hungry.

Our angry generations of children have rebelled against every principle of spirituality and the biblical manual of parenting. Following the example of generations prior, they have played the harlot with the system our government has put in place. I have encountered children who have filed erroneous false reports against their parents who continued to enable them without discipline. The children were either extracted from the home or the parent was arrested with false pretense.

We now have a millennialist generation that has no conscience and we can't figure out why. I'll tell you why. They are an angry generation who has received the aftermath following the self implosion of our immoral culture. Jeremiah 31 in verses 28 through 30, God says:

> 28 Just as I watched over them to uproot and tear down, and to overthrow, destroy and bring disaster, so I will watch over them to build and to plant," declares the LORD. 29 "In those days people will no longer say, 'The fathers have eaten sour grapes, and the children's teeth are set on edge.'

³⁰ Instead, everyone will die for his own sin; whoever eats sour grapes—his own teeth will be set on edge.

God knew the self destruct mode people had embraced in their efforts of removing Him from our culture. He has witnessed it in every empire that has risen to power throughout history, prior to the collapse of the empires. What makes us any different?

I have worked with people in prison for a crime they did not commit. Consider Tom's story. Tom was a lucrative entrepreneur. He had started his own business and did well at work to develop his business. His wife was active in her career as well. Financially they did well; almost too well. They were both confessed Christians and very active in their faith. Tom knew his Bible well from his childhood.

Where Tom had been ensnared by the enemy was in his passive parenting style. Tom had grown up in a society following the Depression and World War II. He knew what it was like to be limited on resources resulting in rations and bartering. Like many of his generation, Tom was committed to be certain his children didn't have to encounter needs and wants in their childhood years like he had to. His kids were in need of nothing throughout their formative years.

Discipline was slack in Tom's household. It didn't take long for his children to learn that at a very early age. In fact, like in the movie "Failure to Launch", Tom's children were so accommodated and undisciplined they never wanted to leave home where life had been so cushy for them to do as they pleased.

Tom's daughter Kathy, at the age of 28 had not only continued living with her parents; she had her drug dealing significant other move in as well. She conceived and gave birth to two more unruly children she refused to discipline. When Kathy was 32, Tom and his wife had had enough and were tired of cleaning up after Kathy and her family. Tom snapped emotionally. With his wife's consent, they both gave Kathy the ultimatum of being out of their house in 30 days or less.

Now this was a girl who had never worked a day in her life. She didn't even cook, wash laundry or clean house.

"And now your kicking me out of the house!!!! ...... You'd better rethink that!!! If you kick me out of this house, both of you will regret it!"

"The ultimatum has not changed. We will be glad to call the police to escort you out if need be!"

"You will pay!!! Boy will you pay!!!!!!!!!!!!"

Two weeks later both Tom and his wife were arrested for a crime they did not commit. Under false pretense, Kathy and her boyfriend told erroneous lies to Child Protective Services that were never even fully investigated. They were accused of sexually molesting their grandchildren.

While incarcerated, both were removed from their own home while Kathy continues to reside there to this day. Tom's son John took over the lucrative business his dad had built from the ground up. He has told his dad he has no intent of giving it back upon Tom's release.

His children are very angry children and as a result they have embraced the "Survival of the Fittest" mentality where the big guy always eats the little guy. In reflection, Tom acknowledged his parenting style was not founded on biblical principles. He looks back and realized he is responsible for the monsters he has created.

Even the military is frustrated with the undisciplined youth we have produced in our culture. Many who become enlisted are unruly youth who have embraced the military because they have exhausted all other options due to their previous behavior. They go into the military ready to manipulate the powers that be just as they did their own parents. Many are let go with a less than honorable or a dishonorable discharge, because they refuse to submit to authority of any kind.

In Exodus 20:12, the fifth of the Ten Commandments is the only commandment with a promise. God said:

> [12] "Honor your father and your mother, so that you may live long in the land the LORD your God is giving you."

Many adult children will not submit to authorities at any level. For that reason, life has not gone well for them. Youth in schools to this day have already been told their projected life span will be shorter than the life span of their parents. Is it any wonder? Lazy, obese, undisciplined people have the deck stacked against them.

We need to return to the disciplines endowed by our Creator since the beginning of time. We need to implement and utilize the biblical principles of parent/child relationships as defined in the manual of parenting; the Bible. Until America wakes up to true biblical parenting of their children, society will remain in its downward spiral of turmoil and degradation.

Many parents are desperate for answers that work in the parenting process. I have gotten calls from clients of parenting until I'm sick of it. I tell all parents struggling in their parenting process, three words: "READ YOUR BIBLE!!!!!!" The Bible is the manual that outlines how we should be the parents God has called us to be.

My heart goes out to the adults who have desperately tried to return to the parents' manual of the Bible but still struggled to implement it because it is something they have never fully been exposed to. A couple had two children ages two and four. The four year old was oppositional at every level in relation to his parents. I sat and observed how they managed his behavior. He began to hurt his two year old sister and both parents caudle the child.

To prevent brother from harming his two year old sister any further, I asked permission of the parents for me to intervene and they granted me the right. I graciously went over to the children, and asked the four year old to come with me. He refused. I then gracefully picked up the four year old and placed him in "The Basket Hold" on my lap and totally disengaged from even recognizing he was there fighting with ever ounce of energy he had to free himself. While the child was flailing, I continued in conversation with the parents who were observing the process.

I demonstrated control of a rebellious child in a non aversive way. As a result, the child had gone limp in my lap after he had wore himself out and I immediately engaged in conversation with the child asking how in the world he ended up on my lap. Three sessions out; harmony in the home was restored. The child's anger had diminished. I got down on the floor with him and we celebrated his new found behaviors together.

I thank God daily for the parenting manual He has given us. I just pray that our culture's eyes are opened to our need to return to the parenting God has called us to. Remember, God has always sent the right person to do the right thing at the right time to impact the right people to serve His purpose. Praise God for His infinite wisdom.

1. When you were a child, what type of a household did you grow up in? Would you have identified it as balanced between nurture and appropriate discipline? If not, take a moment and go around the room for everyone share what their childhood was like and how it has influenced your parenting style.

2. Has anything in culture pulled you away from Godly parenting? If so, what are the things that have crowded God out of your parenting? What can you do to become proactive in developing a godly heritage with your children?

3. When's the first time you realized our culture has been on a slippery slope regarding parenting the next generation? In reflection, when did parenting styles really become squirrely? Why?

4. What are some of the generational differences in the upbringing of the Generation X and the millenialists? What spawned the differences? Have we learned enough from the recent two generations to realize appropriate discipline is essential?

5. How did Tom's lifestyle of parenting compare to you own personal style of parenting? What can you learn from his mistakes?

6. How have cultural shifts impacted your parenting efforts? Will you be able to leave a legacy? Or will you leave this world in despair because you or your parents checked out when you needed the nurture and the discipline was evident?

7. What have we replaced the parenting manual (the Bible) with? Have we resorted to self-help books? What has resulted? Why?

8. What do you think Jeremiah was trying to say in Jeremiah 31:28-30? How have we failed in the parenting process?

9. How does Tom's situation size up to the claims of Dr. Spock who fervently opposed corporal punishment?

10. How did Tom's outcome undermine the foundation of groups who have been disdained with corporal punishment?

11. What gain did material possessions without appropriate disciplines in Tom's story?

12. Many have gone rogue in their childhood years that has spurned their anger, with efforts to resist every authority figure in their life. What has resulted from those who refuse to submit to authority? Give personal input on what each of you have previously witnessed.

Embracing the Dance of Adversity

I memorized II Corinthians 12:6-10 at a very early age. Initially, I had a vague understanding of this passage. As I have shared in the first chapter, I had what I thought would be a life long adversity that I initially thought would plague me until the day I died. Little did I know God had plans to work a miracle in my life as He did.

For those who aren't familiar with II Corinthians 12, the passage speaks of the Apostle Paul when he penned:

> [6]Even if I should choose to boast, I would not be a fool, because I would be speaking the truth. But I refrain, so no one will think more of me than is warranted by what I do or say. [7]To keep me from becoming conceited because of these surpassingly great revelations, there was given me a thorn in my flesh, a messenger of Satan, to torment me. [8]Three times I pleaded with the Lord to take it away from me. [9]But he said to me, **"My grace is sufficient for you, for my power is made perfect in weakness."** Therefore I will boast all the more gladly about my weaknesses, so that Christ's power may rest on me. [10]That is why, for Christ's sake, I delight in weaknesses, in insults, in hardships, in persecutions, in difficulties. **For when I am weak, then I am strong.**

Throughout life, my plea with God to remove my thorn in the flesh was ongoing. I didn't stop after the third time like Paul. Perhaps if I would have embraced the dance of adversity earlier on, that would have expedited God's answer to my prayers more quickly than He did. Perhaps it was a result of me, like Israel, being hard hearted and a stiff necked person.

Let me take you down memory lane to shed some insight of how I dealt with this adverse part of my life and how the Potter patiently shaped and molded me, His clay, into the vessel He has wanted. He continues molding me; an ongoing shaping and defining of my character. "Father, I submit myself and my will totally to You and Your purpose."

I was in 7th grade, when the medicine I was on could no longer contain nor control the seizure activity. I was quickly approaching adolescents and regulating the drug therapy was a roller coaster experience at best. I was sent to a specialist who took me off of Phenobarbital and placed me on a mega dose of Dilantin. I was literally sleeping 18-20 hours per day. I didn't have the ability to function and stay on task much less stay awake.

I was pulled from the public schools I had been in previously due to medical cause. I was tutored by a retired teacher for my entire 7th grade year. Life for me had become extremely adverse. While my classmates were taking pre-algebra and geometry, my tutor was teaching old math or business math as it is identified as today. By the end of my 7th grade year, they had adjusted the meds enough to regain at least a good part of my functionality in the thought process.

When I returned to the scene of the public schools, seizures were manageable but far from controlled. By the time I was a sophomore, I was excited to be able to sign up for theater arts. I have always been attracted to the arts of theater. I was elated when I was one of the students in that class.

What I didn't realize was the fact that I got the easy credit, but the teacher would never take the risk of me on her stage for fear I may seize during performance. That was a risk she refused to take. My adversity was painful for many events in my life when I was looked at differently because of my infirmities.

My junior year I signed up for French class. To gain your diploma at the end of high school, you had to take at least the introductory to a foreign language. Following in my sister's footsteps, I decided to take French as well. We were 5 weeks into the first semester when I seized in French class during the classroom hour.

I was immediately released from that class indefinitely and placed in a study hall for the rest of the semester for an involuntary seizure I had no control over. That teacher, whose name I will spare, had zero tolerance with anyone who had infirmities to the level I did. Today she would be called to task thanks to the class inclusion in our public schools to this day. It is not appropriate to punish a person for what they cannot control.

Now some readers were likely to have been emotionally put out after reading about the atrocities I had to endure through life. Throughout life I was unjustly treated by many a people in my day. Nevertheless, through most of my childhood, I had embraced the Nahum1:1-3 and let God repay with His vengeance rather than placing myself in the Judge's seat. He did just that. My theater arts teacher had a daughter who became epileptic and my French teacher was with child when she expelled me from class. Four months later, she gave birth to a disabled child. God has chastened all of us for our iniquities in His time.

With all of my up hill battles I had to encounter throughout my educational years, I still graduated high school at the age of seventeen, diploma in hand. Being epileptic was what gave me the fortitude to become the tenacious fighter in thought and word ever since. I refused to embrace status quo. God continued to remind me how I was fearfully and wonderfully made; how He knew me and knit me together in my mother's womb. He knew the number of hairs on my head and gave me His unique signature in my finger print that is uniquely different from anyone else. God spares no detail when intricately weaving us together physically, mentally and emotionally. We are made in His image.

I know many readers are scratching their heads right now, wondering how a loving God could even allow and encourage us to embrace the dance with adversities. Read on and hopefully you will be given a glimpse of the necessity of embracing the dances of life with adversity.

Consider the parables of Jesus. A grain of wheat will remain a grain of wheat until it totally surrenders itself and its will to the hands of the Universe Maker. Apart from its surrender to God, it would remain as that and only that; a grain that has extreme potential to make a harvest far beyond its comprehension, but a nonproductive grain nonetheless because it refused to yield itself to its Maker. By itself it can do nothing but in its total surrender to its Maker, it feeds thousands.

Or consider the caterpillar. For months, a caterpillar has one purpose and one goal; eat everything edible that comes my way, from flowers to gardens to fields to leaves from the trees. I am hungry; feed me. Now, when the seasons have reached their matured status, the seasons begin to change and the nights get cooler. God has intricately given the caterpillar a chance for survival even in the midst of one of the coldest winters. Before God will keep that promise of His creation's care, the caterpillar has to totally surrender his life and everything in it to the Master's hands having no idea of the outcome.

In other words, the caterpillar has to have faith in what he cannot see or without question, he will freeze to death. Following his total surrender to the Maker, God intricately takes every caterpillar through the metamorphic state. While in the metamorphic state, God displays His majesty in the artwork at hand. Months later, out emerges a beautiful butterfly that reaffirms God's ever presence in every adverse situation of life.

I have had many adverse situations in life above and beyond of which I will spare you all of the details. There were three adversities I had to embrace the dance with to bring me to where I am in life today. With the reader's patience and permission, I would like to take you back with me down memory lane. Let me share my adult life to gain you perspective of what encouraged me to eventually step out on faith like the caterpillar and surrender everything I had; wife and kids included to the Potter's hands.

I had been in the preaching ministry on and off from full to part time positions throughout my adult life. Many times I had the boldness of Peter and Paul. Other times I waned in my ministry and faith. To address this at a deeper level, God needed my undivided attention. As any minister will tell you, ministry can be very demanding from deadlines that have to be met to people you need to reach out to and oversee, to personal spiritual growth for himself and his family. I had reached an all time low when I shelved personal prayer life and devotions with my Creator. I did this just to accommodate the demands I was attempting to address. Shepherding shut-ins, working with youth, preaching and teaching, not to mention counseling with those who were struggling relationally or from the demons they had previously embraced in life. While serving and worshipping the god of business, I veered off course from what God called me to do for Him and didn't even realize it at the time. I had embraced as normal in ministry to be embracing the struggles and stressors that exacerbated God's purpose for us in ministry. At times, I felt like I was a "Man of the Cloth" and people respected me for who I was. I look back now and see how pharisaic I really was throughout those low points of my ministry career.

Finally, God was sick and tired of me playing church with the gods of time and the gods of prestige. I had forgotten who I was and WHOSE I was. As I reflect back, God must have been so disgusted with my pathetic Christianity. It is likely He even He had turned me over to Satan for a season to get me to come running back to Him. Like Job, I am sure there were many discussions between God and the adversary. God allowed me to be turned over to Satan's hands of adversity to be certain the right person would be ready to do the right thing at the right time to accomplish His purpose.

God allowed me to wander in the wilderness for 10 years I wouldn't even wish on my worst enemy. I was going through the motions of doing church with a hectic schedule and 60 hour weeks when everything literally came to a screeching halt!!!!!! I was driving down the road to stay on task with all the ministries I had established and built up, when I seized behind the wheel and I crashed into an auto dealer's car lot. Talk about being turned over to Satan; this was the ultimate. Fifteen days later my driver's license was suspended indefinitely.

"NOOOOOO! …….. God I don't understand!!!! Have I not dedicated my life to your service with Your people for Your cause? How can you let this happen to your servant?"

You don't have to read much into my response that my faith was pretty shallow at the time. Like many ministers in the faith, I was a micromanagement minister. The only way to do church was my way and I had to be intricately weaved into every ministry of the churches I had worked with prior. I had to be in charge. After all, I had had the college training. I had what no one else had had. (There it was. It was all about *me*! ………. Not about **GOD!**)

As I reflect back, there were many times in my early ministry efforts where I was at question as to why I had never experienced God's presence as I have in recent years. In reflection, the reason I never experienced the presence of God prior was because there was sin in the camp and I was the chief of sinners. Retrospectively, I have yet to figure out why God just didn't wash His hands of me and look for someone else to serve His purpose. But He has pursued me nonetheless, hoping someday I would pursue Him.

The first two years of this life changing experience was like hell on earth. I was angry. I was hostile. I felt I was unjustly treated. At one point I was even angry with God.

"God!!!…. How could you say you love me and then let something like this atrocious event happen to me? I thought you were the Good Shepherd who looked after your sheep."

He graciously listened to my hurt and my pain and my agony, just as He had listened to His Son's when Jesus asked "If at all possible, PLEASE LET THIS CUP PASS FROM ME!" It was painful! How could I bear the weight of the cup God had allowed for me to endure? Yet, not my will, ………. but Thy will be done."

After the third year of this added infirmity, I finally embraced this situation as God's will for my life. It doesn't take a rocket scientist to figure out I was no longer able to remain in ministry. You can't shepherd or make hospital calls without a driver's license. We moved back to my home town community to have support from family and friends. I had to have a support system if I was to survive or even attempt to provide the means of survival for my family. We made do in a makeshift small rental house simply to keep a roof over our head. We remained active in our faith at the Plum Creek Christian Church, a small congregation of about 75 people at the time.

I had finally relented my anger I had kindled against God and others. During the angry phase of this tumultuous transition in my life, I displaced my anger toward my lovely wife who to this day did not deserve it. I have apologized to her profusely ever since. That was a dark place in my life; a place I never want to return to. God had embraced I Corinthians 5 and had briefly turned me over to Satan and the devil had a field day with me.

But like the caterpillar, until I totally surrendered to the will and hands of my Maker, God would not intervene nor impose on my life what I refused to embrace. It took total surrender that occurred in December 2005. Let me describe and define the scenes that precipitated the climactical events that occurred over a nine- month duration.

My neurologist in Indianapolis had exhausted all treatments he had been trained for and the seizures were still far from under control. I had even exhausted medicines that were yet to be FDA approved. Nothing could control the seizures I had to endure. By then, seizures were almost a daily routine event. They would literally drain me from doing anything else the rest of the day. In fact at the time, Laura even had to be my memory because the seizure activity impaired my thought process and memory. I couldn't remember schedules or events or directions. Life was hard.

Finally in the fall of 2005, my neurologist decided to refer me on to the research at the University Of Cincinnati Hospital. We were told up front if an opening becomes available, you need to take it regardless. It needs to be priority one. Wouldn't you know it, they wanted me there right around Christmas of 2005. We were told it would be likely I would be held through the holiday. Regardless, all family members encouraged me to take it. So I embraced the dance of adversity. The only one who was anxious about my embracing the dance with adversity was our oldest son, John Thomas. When we had our family discussion regarding the pros and cons of embracing this dance with adversity, he said, "Dad, I want what's best for you, but I'm afraid if you go through this surgery you might not even remember us anymore." We shared in the same pains together and he too relinquished me to the "The Potter's hands". It was truly a leap of faith for our children.

For nine months I went through a series of tests. I was poked and prodded so much that I felt like a pin cushion. Finally, the neurologists said they had all the information they needed to determine whether I would be candidate for lobectomy, accept one final test that would require surgery before the primary surgery. They said, "We would like to crack your skull to place a plate right on the surface of the brain to pin point where the seizure activity is, but we need your consent." In total surrender to the Great Physician, we encouraged them to do what they had to do.

I was anesthetized. They did what they had to do. When they were finished, I had a massive headache that migraines can't even touch. Morphine was my best friend when they were putting me through the final test. In 48 hours they had all the information they needed. They held a medical team conference and concluded I was a patient that truly qualified for lobectomy.

They came to the room to talk with both my wife and I. They said, "Well, we have some good news and some bad news."

"Okay. Let's hear the bad news first."

"Well it has been determined you have seizure activity on both sides of the brain. We think the left hemisphere is triggering the right hemisphere to seize. We can only remove one side not both."

"So what is your recommendation?"

"Well, we would like to remove the damaged portion of the left hemisphere and hopefully that will alleviate the seizure activity in the right hemisphere."

"What are the risks?"

"Well, you could lose your peripheral vision on your left side. You could lose your short term memory; your speech could become partially impaired. And as in every surgery you could die. We will give you and your wife time to talk about it and we will come back in a couple of hours to see what you decide."

Laura and I locked eyes as they left the room. I said, "We need to pray!" She agreed so I began to pray. For the first time in my life, I literally experienced my faith. As I was praying, there was a peace that filled the entire room. It was such the experience that I could never define it with words. It was as though God was in that room with us like never before. It was awesome to embrace the dance with our Creator like we had never experienced before.

When I finished praying, Laura then prayed, seeking God's face and His will for my life and our future. When she finished, my eyes engaged with hers, "Did you notice anything different as we were actively seeking His will?"

"Yes! It was a peace like I have never encountered before."

"We need to do this! I may become a vegetable, but if it serves His purpose, we will remain in His will none the less." She turned me over to the hands of the "Great Physician" and when the doctors returned to the room we signed the papers and submitted to the will of our Heavenly Father. I didn't know what the future held for me, but I know who held the future in the palm of His hands. Like the caterpillar, I surrendered my all to the God of the Universe as He took me through the metamorphic process. God couldn't use me until I trusted Him in total surrender.

Aren't we all guilty of that to some extent? "God, I'll go through the motions every Sunday, but I will manage my own affairs the rest of the week, while I have you placed in the small box on the mantle. I don't have time for you this week God. When things slow down for me and deadlines are no longer breathing down my neck, I'll make time for You then."

Sometimes God will step back and remove His presence from you. He may allow the tormentor to embrace the dance with you, where calamity upon calamity begins to overwhelm you. We begin to wonder why all of this is happening to me? In reflection over when all the calamities began, was immediately following your lack of time to embrace the dances God has called you to. Because He was no longer priority one, He briefly removed Himself from you like the father of the prodigal son.

The father of the prodigal never followed the son pleading with him to "Please! Don't go!!!" The father prematurely gave the son his inheritance. It was as though the son was saying, "Dad, you are dead to me! I no longer want to be called your son! I want to go out into the world and actually experience life on my own. You are stifling me! I have only one life to live and I am not going to waste it on you!!!!!!!!!!" And the father let the son go; knowing the pain his son would soon encounter. He let him go nonetheless.

I would venture the father of the prodigal tearfully turned his son over to the adversary, rather than insisting his son experience the same faith he had experienced. I believe God does the same with us when we refuse to embrace our genuine relationship with our Maker. Either you are all in or you are completely removed from God's presence. There is no middle ground.

The father knew he had to release the son to adversities to hopefully get him so broken that he would come running back to his father. God allows us to experience adversities to get us to come running back to His will and His purpose. Aside from Jesus Himself, all have played the prodigal at one point or another, just as I had. It wasn't until I came running back to God in total surrender that He began to literally move mountains in my life. It has been an awesome thing to embrace ongoing dances with a limitless King. "Lead on God! Lead on!"

With prep time and recovery time included, the surgeons had forecasted it would be a 4-5 hour procedure but the family would be kept up to date as things progressed. I was waiting for prep time when the phone rang. Dr. David L. Eubanks, of Johnson Bible College, had been following my case and he called me to share with and pray for me and God's guidance of the surgeon's hands. Wow!!!!! The president called?!!!!!!! I was floored to hear the voice of the president. President Eubanks was a genuine servant of God's and he prayed for me and my family that day. The peace we experienced prior was felt a second time. That was God's affirmation as to say, "And low I am with you always."

I am grateful our minister from Plum Creek, Rory Christenson was there that day. Prior to surgery, he prayed for us as well and agreed to attempt to watch over our three kids as they waited for the completion of the surgery. While under the knife, Rory kept the boys occupied with video games on his laptop. His wife called near the halfway point to see how things were going. Rory's response? "Things are great! The boys and I are conquering the world on my laptop." His distraction to and for our children was appreciated more than he will ever know.

The 4-5 hours past and the surgery was far from over. Laura's anxiety began to escalate and she resorted to prayer more than once. Six hours had passed; no update. Seven, then eight hours past. There was still no word from the doctor or nurses. God was working with my entire family that day. God was asking them again and again, "Can you trust Me?........ Can you fully relinquish your husband/father/son/brother to Me and My will?" They all affirmed me to His sovereign will.

By the end of the ninth hour, the surgeon came out to tell the family and informed them about the success of the surgery. He then called Laura with one other to meet with him in the conference room. Our daughter, Tabitha said, "I'm going!" She had always been daddy's little princess.

In the conference room, they affirmed the success of the surgery but they ran into some complications. They said the brain is three and a half pounds of a firm mass. When they got into the brain they saw a mass of the brain that was like mush. They said, "He never did use that part of the brain. Your brain is a lot like a computer. The other parts of the brain would send a signal to the damaged mass. When it failed to respond to the initial signal sent, like a computer, John would shut down, seize, and reboot the computer process. We were all totally amazed John had as high level of functionality as he did. He should be okay once he has recovered from the anesthetic. All of his vitals are okay, he should be fine. It will take about 6-8 weeks for the recovery process to be complete and it will take every bit of a year to totally recover from the trauma to the brain but he should be fine."

Another hour passed before I came to. Ow! Ow! Ow! Ow! Ow! Morphine or not, I was in a pain that was so excruciating they never created words to define the intensity of it. I couldn't even stand light. Everyone's normal talk was like a high decibel sound that provoked the pain to an even more intense level. "Where's the morphine!!!! I Need It Now!!!"

"We have given you the maximum dose we can give you at this time. You'll have to wait another two hours before we can give you anymore. Would you like us to bring your wife in?"

"Sure!"

She came in and we embraced. Laura was so relieved God had spared me in the surgical process. We talked with one another about the pain level, how the memory was still intact, speech was unaffected and my peripheral vision had not been impaired. Laura then suggested we really needed to bring John Thomas (also known as J.T.) into the room to show that God had truly spared his dad. When Laura left to get him, she escorted him in my room and the first words out of my mouth were, "J.T., I know who you are".

His response? "Thank you God, for bringing my dad through the surgery."

God was shining down on my family that day like never before. He probably would never have shined as He did had I not fully surrendered everything I had to Him in the metamorphic process. When He saw I had no other gods before Him and I submitted everything to Him I had, He began moving mountains in my life like never before.

"Thank you Lord, for encouraging me to embrace the dance with adversities that taught me to include and submit to your will in every part of my life. You miraculously healed me that day of the infirmities I had encountered for 42 years of my life."

I even told the specialist at my first follow up appointment. "I don't want to discredit your profession and training because all of you do good work. However, on the day of my surgery, your hands were guided by the Great Physician. The specialist agreed.

I am now 47 and God has kept me seizure free ever since. God touched me in a way that started me on an entirely new path in my adult life. My driver's license was reinstated 16 months later. I have had energy to burn. Five to six hours of sleep is all I need now that

I am drug and seizure free. My memory is now sharper than it has ever been. I am an entirely new creation that God has touched in a unique way to serve His purpose in my life.

The pain level immediately following surgery was a fifteen of ten. It was excruciatingly painful. By the time they released me to return home for my six to eight week recovery, the pain had only diminished to a 10 of 10. After the first week, over night the pain divinely diminished to a one of ten. If I had to do it over again, I would do it in a heartbeat. The painful encounter with the end result was priceless.

My health was restored. My career was restored. My family was completely restored. Everything I had lost had been restored to me by the sovereign Lord. I made it through the metamorphic process under the care of the One I had surrendered to.

Most everyone faces trials of many kinds. Those trials temper us to the strength we need to have to sustain us through life's challenges that lie ahead. We all have valley experiences that follow our mountain top experiences in life. When we face the pains of the valley, we need to remember, the valley is where we receive the nutrients that we need to sustain us for the next mountain top experiences in life.

On both the mountain top and in the valleys of life, it is imperative to remember that God is sovereign to restore His faithful to the mountain top experiences, either in this life or in life eternal. Even the disciples were willing to suffer for their faith in Christ. Why should we be any different? Whether persecuted or not, until we can fully submit in faith to the spiritual metamorphic process of the Creator's hands, it is difficult to reach the potential God wants us to reach to serve His purpose for our lives.

1. What is the greatest adversity God has allowed to exist in your personal life that has tempered you with time? Explain.

2. What are your thoughts about the grain that had potential verses the one who embraced the total surrender of self to the sovereign will of God? How should that compare to our willingness to Embrace the Dance with Adversity?

3. Is your faith strong enough you can believe that which remains unseen? Or are you one who talks the talk; but can't walk the walk by surrendering to the Master's hands?

4. Has God ever needed your undivided attention when you encountered trials of many kinds? What resulted? Did you submit to His sovereign will? Why or why not?

5. On a scale of one to ten, where would you gauge your spiritual walk right now? How does that compare to your life previous?

6. Has selfishness and being self absorbed ever tripped you up? What was the outcome? Is it something you would want to do again? Why?

7. Did your adversity in life lead you to question the reality of a loving God? Have you found reconciliation with God? Or are you still at odds with Him?

8. What can we learn from Jesus' total surrender to the will of the Potter? Haven't we been called to do the same?

9. Have you ever displaced your anger out toward ones who genuinely love you? What did that do to the relationship? How did you seek reconciliation?

10. Is prayer a vibrant staple of your daily living or do you have a history of only calling on God in crisis? Have you considered developing that part of your spiritual walk further? What are some ways you can?

11. When has painful experiences in your life strengthened your character? What resulted?

12. When your family has been in adverse situations, for whatever reason, did it strengthen or weaken the family dynamic? Why?

Embracing the Dance with Rebellion

Rebellion existed prior to the Creation of this vast universe we now live in. Isaiah 14 gives us a snapshot of what happened in Heaven when he wrote in chapter 14:

> ¹² How you have fallen from heaven,
> O morning star, son of the dawn!
> You have been cast down to the earth,
> you who once laid low the nations!

> ¹³ You said in your heart,
>   "I will ascend to heaven;
>   I will raise my throne
>   above the stars of God;
>   I will sit enthroned on the mount of assembly,
>   on the utmost heights of the sacred mountain. [c]

> ¹⁴ I will ascend above the tops of the clouds;
>   I will make myself like the Most High."

> ¹⁵ But you are brought down to the grave,
>   to the depths of the pit.

> ¹⁶ Those who see you stare at you,
>   they ponder your fate:
>   "Is this the man who shook the earth
>   and made kingdoms tremble,

¹⁷ the man who made the world a desert,
    who overthrew its cities
    and would not let his captives go home?"

Satan was one of the archangels who served and worshipped his Creator just as we have been called to do. But just like Lucifer, many of us puff up with pride saying,"Look at me! Look at what I did!" And again Satan lures us away from the will of God just as he did the Pharisees and Sadducees of Jesus' day. They had studied the Pentateuch and the prophets of old and they considered themselves to be men of the cloth. They were too religious and too righteous to be wrong. What they failed to realize was the fact that anyone and everyone can be religious, yet at the same time religiously wrong. Even God's chosen can be religiously wrong.

Noah was a drunk. Moses was a murderer. Isaac and Jacob had dysfunctional families. David was an adulterer and a murderer. Sampson was a womanizer. Solomon had a harem of 300 wives and 700 concubines. Jonah tried to flee the call the Creator had called him to. Paul previously persecuted the Church and the Christians until his road to Damascus. He was even present when Stephen was stoned to death for his faith. Most of God's creation has rebelled against Him and His precepts at one point or another. It may be to the extreme as it was with the prodigal son or it may be a gradual hardening of the heart to manmade tradition and practice of worship. Maybe it was when we blended the Old and New Testament at our church building and we made the sanctuary in the church building the Holy of Holy's and have forbidden laughter or anything else in the sanctuary aside from solemnest even to the point of comparing it to a funeral dirge. I have never been inspired by dead churches steeped in tradition.

Even I rebelled against God's will. Now before you become too critical, Paul wrote to the church in Rome "²³For all have sinned, and come short of the glory of God." I was the Jonah who fled to Tarshish when God called me to preach at Nineveh. I thought I could run from God. (Pretty stupid, don't you think?) Besides, there was a great deal of promise at the Tarshish I fled to. I will change the names of the places and ministries to protect the names and the people involved.

After starting my private practice in Christian counseling, things became financially tight the first couple of years. Any entrepreneur will tell you when you begin a business, it is not uncommon to lose money into the business the first year or so. That is one of the costs of the birthing process of a new business. To accommodate the financial need God had called me back into the preaching ministry with First Church that was only 25 miles away from where I lived. Now remember, I had been removed from the preaching ministry for an entire decade when we embraced the dance with adversity. I was rusty to say the least. I had supply preached there a couple times already and they really didn't seem too excited at First Church to really want to grow. It was like they were quite content with their god in a box that they would remove once a week. "God, what's the purpose in that? …. Why go to Nineveh where the sin is great and they don't want to change anyway? ……………… Not interested God. Send someone else. Besides, I have been offered a good paying job in a counseling ministry in the southern part of the state. I don't have time to preach at a church right now." There the evil word surfaced again……… the word "I".

In retrospect, I had a great deal of commonalities with Jonah. God had set me apart for the ministry to impact the world around me with the truths of the Gospel. God has had His plans to use me in many churches and many ministries, most of which I am very grateful for. But I couldn't embrace ministry to a dying church. They had a history of splitting twice. They had at one point had over 200 in attendance. One split resulted from an accident that had occurred on a hayride one fall. One of the children fell off and went under the wheel of the hay wagon and was injured. The family of the child who was hurt sued the church for damages. Satan had ensnared the entire church into a tumultuous upheaval with the legal system. Rather than seeking God's face and His direction on this matter, they polarized into groups of opposition within the church.

God turned them over to Satan and Satan split the church right down the middle. Now First Church had split into First and Second

Church. Satan has used that maneuver throughout the history of the church. And we have embraced the dance with rebellion and have splintered the church and the power of Christ into many factions of denominationalism. The most important factor to all involved was the fact that "I" was right! And you may have won the battle but you lost the war if that in the least way defines you. There is no room for "I" in any of Christ's church.

Years later, the First Church, now only having 85 on average, was doing their best to limp before God after being turned over to Satan for a season. Hind sight is always 20/20. They were still licking their wounds from their previous dance with the devil. They had experienced emotional wounds that ran deep. Many had elected to transfer their anger to bitterness toward the other group who had split from them and there were dissensions in the camps.

A new minister, still wet behind the ears, embraced First Church in an effort to restore the unity of the church. The First Church welcomed him with opened arms with their sites on restoration of Christ's church. The minister was very waxed and poised in his ability to work with people. He was able to woo people back to Christ and he impacted a great deal of people and Satan didn't like it.

Understanding the minister's undisciplined relationships with people, the devil lured the minister into a spiritual trap of a sexual affair with one of the women of the church. Once again, God turned them over to Satan as they played the harlot. Dissensions escalated again, the church polarized again and you guessed it, they split again. Now we have First church, Second Church and Third church all within a 4 mile radius. Each one of them had been rendered powerless.

Satan was at his zenith in this given county I had been called to preach at. Like Nineveh, this community had played the harlot. They may have won a battle here and there, but it was evident, they had lost the spiritual war. Now God is calling me to preach to the Ninevites of First Church and I said, "NO!" I embraced the dance of rebellion against my Creator even after He had restored me completely. If I could go back in time in a time machine, I would have cried out "Yes Lord! Let's set sail together." But I was too absorbed in what "I" wanted to do rather than on what God called me to do. And God turned me over to Satan and Satan had a field day with that year.

Like the Pharisees and Sadducees, I justified my actions with religious argument. After all, I had been called to ministry with a Christian Counseling Ministry in Southern Indiana that really looked promising. I'd start out on a 90 day trial accommodated with an affordable stipend and if they liked what they saw in the 90 day trial, they would set up a contract with sizable pay for my ministry services there.

Satan made certain my eyes were blinded to the narcissistic personality of the owner of the business masked as a ministry. I was embracing the dance of rebellion with wolves in sheep's clothing. I engaged in the dance. With blinders still on, I never questioned the discrepancies between what I was promised to be paid and what I actually received. Like the Pharisees, I was constantly justifying their actions. "They've hit a rough patch. They will still make it right."

Satan continued to lure me to the point where I was sleeping in a tent 75 miles from my family, 75 miles from my church family and I felt like Satan had me in the center of the coliseum where he was mocking me as powerless and worthless. I was expendable at every level. I had been swallowed by the great fish just as Jonah had been when he rejected God's call. I'm certain there was some serious replaying in Jonah's mind of where, when and why Jonah had rebelled against the Creator of the universe.

While bathing in the digestive tract and enzymes of this smelly fish, he had resigned to life as he once knew it. He replayed the tapes in his memory of what he had just encountered while on the ship headed to Tarshish. Let's look at the replay of events in Jonah 1, beginning with verse 1.

> [1] The word of the LORD came to Jonah son of Amittai: [2] "Go to the great city of Nineveh and preach against it, because its wickedness has come up before me."

> [3] **But Jonah ran away from the LORD** and headed for Tarshish. He went down to Joppa, where he found a ship bound for that

port. After paying the fare, he went aboard and sailed for Tarshish to flee from the LORD.

⁴ Then the LORD sent a great wind on the sea, and such a violent storm arose that the ship threatened to break up. ⁵ All the sailors were afraid and each cried out to his own god. And they threw the cargo into the sea to lighten the ship.

But Jonah had gone below deck, where he lay down and fell into a deep sleep. ⁶ The captain went to him and said, "How can you sleep? Get up and call on your god! Maybe he will take notice of us, and we will not perish."

⁷ Then the sailors said to each other, "Come, let us cast lots to find out who is responsible for this calamity." They cast lots and the lot fell on Jonah.

⁸ So they asked him, **"Tell us, who is responsible for making all this trouble for us? What do you do? Where do you come from? What is your country? From what people are you?"**

⁹ He answered, "I am a Hebrew and I worship the LORD, the God of heaven, who made the sea and the land."

¹⁰ This terrified them and they asked, **"What have you done?" (They knew he was running away from the LORD, because he had already told them so.)**

¹¹ The sea was getting rougher and rougher. So they asked him, "What should we do to you to make the sea calm down for us?"

¹² "Pick me up and throw me into the sea," he replied, "and it will become calm. I know that it is my fault that this great storm has come upon you."

¹³ **Instead, the men did their best to row back to land. But they could not, for the sea grew even wilder than before. ¹⁴ Then they cried to the LORD, "O LORD, please do not let us die for taking this man's life. Do not hold us accountable for killing an innocent man, for you, O LORD, have done as you pleased."** ¹⁵ Then they took Jonah and threw him overboard, and the raging sea grew calm. ¹⁶ **At this the men greatly feared the LORD, and they offered a sacrifice to the LORD and made vows to him.**

¹⁷ But the LORD provided a great fish to swallow Jonah, and Jonah was inside the fish three days and three nights.

God can intervene and use even the most rebellious when He sees opportunity. So he created a storm that was powerful enough o capsize and or break the ship in half. Rebellious Jonah fell into a deep sleep and the sailors had to wake him up pleading to pray to his god as they had been doing, hoping the gods would have mercy on them. They each prayed to their own gods.

Don't we do the same thing in our churches? We pray to our god of time. We worship the god of career, the god of tradition, the god of habits. And we wonder why the church is ready to close the doors. We wonder why God turns them over to Satan for a season. That is when God will orchestrate the rebellious to still serving His purpose. There were people in need of parenting skills, strained marriages, depression, anxiety attacks and the like; people whose lives God touched through His efforts there. But he wasn't finished with me yet.

God removed my blinders I had been wearing in my pious rebellion against the will of God. By the time the blinders were removed, I had almost lost everything I ever had, again; .... my house, my car, my phone was disconnected and the electric was turned off. God had even sent other minister's in my life who attempted to remove my blinders earlier to the Narcissist I had contracted with.

With that in mind, it kind of reminds me of the tale about the frog and the scorpion. The scorpion had come to a river bank and needed to cross to the other side. He struck up a conversation with the amphibious frog hoping to get the frog to swim the scorpion across the river. The frog resisted the scorpion, suggesting the scorpion would strike him with the deadly poison in his tail while amidst the water and swim. The scorpion replied, "I promise I will surely not strike you with my tail; you are my friend and my confidant. Why would I strike a friend swimming to where I need to go?" The frog finally consented and reluctantly began the swim with the scorpion on his back. When the frog got to the other side with the scorpion in tow, the scorpion got off of the back of the frog, turned in front of him face to face and thanked the frog for the voyage as he was striking the frog with his tail. The frog cried out, "How could you strike one you called your friend and confidant! I will surely perish now!" The scorpion replied narcissistically, "Because, it is my nature." And he walked away from the dying frog.

I was the frog in the contract and I had embraced the dance of rebellion against **my** God. And Satan struck because it was his nature. He brought **my** empire to a screeching halt. That word surfaces daily and like Paul, I have to remind myself daily as he did in I Corinthians 15:9-11. Paul wrote:

> [9]For I am the least of the apostles and do not even deserve to be called an apostle, because I persecuted the church of God. [10]But by the grace of God I am what I am, and his grace to me was not without effect. No, I worked harder than all of them—yet not I, but the grace of God that was with me. [11]Whether, then, it was I or they, this is what we preach, and this is what you believed.

I am least of the ministers of the gospel. I have to buffet myself daily and die to myself everyday sometimes multiple times a day; not to become a martyr but to discipline myself from the sin of puffed up pride. After my encounter of rebellion against the Creator of the universe, I went running, not walking, back into the arms of God and He restored Me to His purpose. The invitation was still open at First Church. I embraced the ministry and embraced the call for 18 months. God restored our financial support. We embraced the dance with God once again and He was awesome.

Thank you Lord, for being the "God of a second chance and the God of grace". I would have perished in the great fish without you.

1. When rebellion was first witnessed, what preceded it? What had it resulted from?

2. In reflection and with a gracious spirit toward others in the group, tell about when you rebelled most against God's will for your life. What resulted? What drew you back to God's will?

3. How have churches in your community been ravaged by the adversary like the first church in this chapter?

4. When was the last time dissension was evidenced in the church family you worshipped with? Was it handled and addressed biblically or secularly? What resulted?

5. When was the last time you became self focused and said "No!" when God called you to his purpose? Being the gentleman he is, how did he respond? What events followed your refusal?

6. What calamities, if any, resulted from your rebellious response to God's call?

7. Just as Jonah had time to reflect over his past, while in the great fish, when you had time to reflect on your Jonah experiences, what came into perspective as a result?

8. How did God give you a second chance? What was your response?

9. As all the men on the boat cried out to their own gods, what gods throughout time have you cried out to when trials have come your way?

10. Like the narcissist referred to in this chapter, when was the last time you had an encounter with the scorpion? What resulted?

11. What had to occur to in your situation before you realized you served a God of a second chance? What was your response?

12. How were you humbled to run back into the arms of God after the rebellious encounter?

Embracing the Dance of Total Surrender

As presented in the first chapter, I was brought up in a rural community in south eastern Indiana. Fields and livestock was the means of living. County and state fairs were a big thing in Indiana. I had a cousin who showed registered Angus every year at the fair. Curious as I was, one year, I finally asked him how he tamed a 2000 pound beast to submit to his leading it around the show barn before the judges at the fair. He said, "That's easy! Do you see that mule over there? I take my calves at a very early age and yoke them up with that mule twice their size. They will wear themselves out in their struggle with the mule who refuses to go anywhere he doesn't want to go. Their rebellious spirit is broken and they finally surrender their own will to go wherever the mule or I want them to go."

I thought, "Man, that will preach! …….. When we refuse to be in total surrender to our Creator, we realistically wear ourselves out just like the 2000 pound beast, we fight and resist our Creator until we literally wear ourselves out!"

Total surrender is rarely supported in our American culture these days. Culturally we are taught to be assertive with an attitude of entitlement. Like the grasshopper who cried out "The world owes me a living! Tra! La! La! La! La! La! La!" while he watched the ant labor all summer long. We feel justified and entitled to a free lunch so we are always opened to hand outs that society will grant us. Defiantly against God and against all authorities, we have embraced the dance of defiance rather than the dance of surrender. As a result we have second and third generation welfare recipients who refuse to work or receive training to move forward in life for fear they will lose their food stamps and welfare check. They will ask, "Why should we work when the government will write us a check every month?"

Throughout all of history every empire would rise and then fall because of the apathy and the welfare given them by the government. Corruption, selfishness and greed always preceded the collapse of every empire throughout history. It doesn't take a rocket scientist to see where the United States is currently at in the international scene.

Our culture in America today reminds me of the story about the Little Red Hen retold by many authors. The Little Red Hen lived on a quaint little farm. There also lived on this quaint little farm a cat, a rat, a mouse and a pig. The Little Red Hen was a very industrious creature. Every spring, summer and fall of the year, she was a hard worker.

The Little Red Hen, use to be a good moral that served our country well for decades. But we left that standard when we encouraged citizens to milk the system and let the government take care of them. Rather than totally surrendering themselves and everything they have to their Creator, they surrender themselves to their entitled check every month and we are now into second and third generation recipients of the welfare system. What most of them fail to realize is they have become ensnared in their thinking and they are subject to the government's care. Many never reach their fullest potential in life because of the entrapment they have embraced with welfare.

Many welfare recipients will resort to pushing street drugs as their secondary income. Others resort to organized crime because there is no paper trail and without a paper trail there are no taxes paid. There can be a great deal of money to be made in the drug arena. Working in the prison system, I have been exposed to many of the tactics drug dealers have utilized to make their living. In the prison walls, cell phones are contraband and no staff is allowed to take a cell phone in. Yet months into my work there, there was a big drug bust on the other side of the state being run by a drug lord from inside the facility I was working. He had bought a cell phone for $850.00 that had been smuggled in by a dirty corrections officer.

People like that throughout our society refuse to embrace the dance with total surrender to God. They are convinced they can beat the system. They will do whatever they want whenever they want and they will submit to no one. For a time, their rebelliousness appears to be working for them; fast cash, carousing the bars all night long, more women than any man would ever want at one time. Sexual encounter after sexual encounter. Talk about the life. They demand life on their terms and God turns them over as defined again in Romans 1:18-32.

Then reality hits. Under close observation and gathering of evidence, police are led to a drug bust and multiple people are arrested for the choices they embraced in life on their terms. Not only are they incarcerated, many drug dealers experience withdraw symptoms when they can't get their fix. They go through detoxification and join AA or NA to gain group support for the choices and consequences that have occurred.

Once they have been cleaned up, many will reflect over the poor choices they made and often times they are emotionally and mentally broken like the Angus calves I wrote about at the beginning of the chapter. In the past three years at the prison facility, worship services and Bible studies are mushrooming through the facility. Some of them have even had prayer vidules for other struggling offenders. The power of God has been witnessed by many in the prison setting. It is a field white unto harvest.

Often everyone falls on hard times in life. I am convinced God allows us to have those hard times when we wander from His will for our lives. We rebelliously defy Him with our stiff necked self-will. God steps back and removes Himself from our presence. Life on our own may seem to start out okay but then things become squirrely when we continue down that path apart from God's divine plan for us.

Consider the life of Mark. Mark was a lucrative public servant in his community. He was on staff at the fire station as one of the top firefighters. He was active in his faith and attended worship routinely. He didn't only go through the motions, he experienced his faith. He was consistently devoted to his wife as a one-woman-man and was the proud father of 2.

Mark was an all or nothing type person and he devoted his efforts to anything he participated in. He helped to start a cadet program to troubled teens who needed mentoring and possible training to become the next generation of fire fighters. The cadet program sky rocketed on demand of his time and efforts made. It became nothing uncommon for church and family taking second place to the new cadet program that was being utilized. In fact, it even invaded his time and investments into his faith walk with His Creator. Mark stopped going to church because he was too busy being the humble servant of his community.

Then it happened. He was accused of sexual misconduct with a minor; one he had been working with in the cadet program. Mark had spoken sexually with the minor and touched her inappropriately. The charges were pressed because Mark had allowed himself to be put in a bad spot with this girl apart from the presence of any other witnesses which made everything Mark said, hearsay. Hearsay will never hold up in court.

Mark caught two cases against him by the Fire Chief who decided to make a public spectacle of Mark. With his anxiety reaching an elevated level of being a 12 of 10, and his depression level being an 8 of 10, Mark sought counsel. In reflection, Mark acknowledged, things really started to become squirrely when he stopped having time for God, church and family. Mark said, "It was great when I was actively in the will of God, serving his community. But when I drifted from my commitment and total surrender to God, the blessings stopped and the chaos of my life began to wreak havoc."

Mark recognized he had strayed from the will of God with his business in life. Mark is convinced this was God's way of calling him back to where God wants Mark to serve His purpose, in His impeccable timing. Mark embraced the struggles of his predicament by repenting to his Heavenly Father and totally surrendering everything he had to the Creator of the universe.

Upon his total surrender to God, six weeks later things started to be restored to Mark one at a time. Like Joseph of the Old Testament, Mark has learned to bloom in his faith wherever God places him, which is currently in the prison system. As a result, Mark has impacted hundreds of lives in the facility he is currently in. Mark said, "I have learned to keep God as priority one in my life and the relationship with my wife is second to it."

Total surrender can be very painful. Like the cardiologist who comes into the office after the tests have been run. He informs you that you are lucky to be alive with the blockage you currently have. Unless you consider a stent or a bypass, you are likely to have a heart attack in the next 12-18 months.

Most readers would immediately consider the surgery as imperative. Many would be willing to sign the necessary papers and endure the excruciating pain necessary to be granted a little more time with family and friends. They would surrender their lives and their own well being into the hands of the surgeon.

So why is it so difficult for us to surrender our own well being to the Great Physician and His will for our lives? He has told us throughout scripture that apart from His will and apart from His divine purpose, we have no hope and are condemned to eternal death in hell. God wants what is best for all of us. He has blessings for all of us that we never receive because of our rebellious stiff necked refusal to surrender.

We get so caught up in the comforts of this world that the enemy gets us to focus on self rather than the Great Commission Jesus called us to. Even in our Bible Colleges, we have overlooked our calling to the hurting and the poor. We have glossed over Jesus' phrase in Matthew 19:20-22, when he was approached by the rich young ruler. Like the rich young ruler, many of us sorrowfully turn away from God's calling because giving up our comfort and family is too high of a price to pay.

I have even been in church settings where they refused to allow people to preach unless they had been to a Bible College that had trained them. They had overlooked the fact that the disciples and prophets of old were common ordinary men. They failed to acknowledge that Jesus was known to commune and meet with the sinners and publicans in their world as they knew it.

Churches, ministers of the gospel and elders have embraced their levels of comfort in the church setting just as the Pharisees and Sadducees of Jesus' day. They have held to the idea that comfort is what will draw the people to Christ. We get so caught up in the materialistic church that has become the greatest in size that we limit our influence to one community rather than embracing the Great Commission which calls us to go into the entire world.

Many have reduced themselves to serving a god they can be comfortable with rather than surrendering everything they have to the cause of Christ. Like everything else, we have to be able to control and manipulate our goals and purposes in life to be happy and content; even if it means controlling our destiny in this world.

Yahweh is Greater than that! He has a purpose for everyone who has embraced His purpose in total surrender to His cause. God has called all of us to visit the sinners in their world. He has called us to feed the hungry. He has called us to minister to the poor. He has called us to visit those in prison and to those who are held captive. He has called us to minister to the broken hearted.

Instead of embracing total surrender to God's calling, many have embraced higher education as their platform. I am not writing against higher education. I am simply suggesting we have our priorities out of synch with God's calling. We have relied on our own understanding rather than allowing ourselves to be prompted by the Holy Spirit. As a result many rarely experience the prompting of the Holy Spirit as it was intended to be.

I hope all readers will not only get their priorities in order for life, but I hope it has become more evident that total surrender to God is imperative for living life in this world the way He wants us to. God wants us to freely desire to dance with Him. Satan does everything he can to thwart the dances God calls us to. And he has ensnared all of us at one point or another. The dancing with God in life can only be attained through embracing the dance with total surrender, not partial surrender. God may have to send the right person at the right time to say the right thing that will get us to totally surrender everything to His sovereign will for our lives. So I encourage every reader, it is imperative to embrace the dance with total surrender.

1. Why is surrender so foreign to the people of our culture?

2. How has defiance to authority permeated our culture here in America in the past generations?

3. Why throughout history have generations made every effort to beat the system? Why is it so foreign for our culture to embrace total submission to the will of someone else?

4. What is so attractive about the bad boys and bad girls of our day? Why do people want to instill assertiveness rather than total submission?

5. Why is it so much easier for us to endure the pain of a by-pass surgery than it is to endure the pain of surrender? Both allow us to live better and longer, yet we genuinely struggle when we encounter the pains of surrender. Why is that so difficult?

6. So why is it so difficult for us to surrender our own well being to the Great Physician and His will for our lives?

7. We get so caught up in the comforts of this world that the enemy gets us to focus on self rather than the Great Commission Jesus called us to. So what can we do to be prepared when the adversary attempts to take our focus off of Jesus?

8. In surrender, we are to live life a day at a time in total surrender to God's sovereign will. In his model prayer, Jesus prayed, "…... give us this day our daily bread." Why did he word it that way?

9. Why are we not allowing members of the church serve at every capacity as defined in scripture? Why have we limited ministry to the minister?

10. What limits the gifts God so richly wants to bless us with? Why?

11. How have so many gotten caught up in the comfort of a materialistic church that simply ministers to their own rather than truly Embracing the Dance of Surrender to his Great Commission he commissioned us to?

12. Why does Jesus call us to a total surrender? Why did Jesus ask the rich young ruler to sell everything he had and give it to the poor?

Embracing the Dance with Restoration

Before readers can fully embrace the dance with restoration, there must first be an infirmity to be restored from. As stated by John Maxwell, "Every miracle in the Bible was preceded by a problem. If you have a problem, you are candidate for a miracle; if you have no problem, too bad!" God never succumbed to being a genie in a bottle just waiting to answer our every beckon call when we want something. After hearing that from John Maxwell, I realized I was genuinely a candidate for just that; a miracle.

Now throughout most of my Christian life, I had always been taught miracles only happened in Bible times; from the creation to the flood to the parting of the Red Sea. God was among His people in the wilderness as a cloud during the day and as a pillar of fire by night. God brought manna and quail to feed this stiff necked generation of Abraham's seed.

God went before the Israelites when they conquered the Promised Land, save the first battle at Ai, because there was sin in the camp. Achan was the guilty party that surfaced after 56 warriors had been slain resulting from his sin. Joshua ordered both Achan and his entire household to be stoned to death. Joshua went back to God in prayer asking "Are we good now?" And God returned to help them defeat the enemies in Canaan. Every miracle in the Old Testament was preceded by a problem.

Even in the New Testament, Jesus performed miracles throughout His entire ministry; all the way from turning water into wine to raising dead men who had been dead for two days. He healed the blind man and the leper. He raised the lame to his feet. He healed the woman whose flowing was stopped. He fed the hungry and gave living water to those who were thirsty for righteousness. He calmed the waters of a raging sea. He found coins in the fish's mouth. He has healed the broken hearted and down trodden.

Jesus then passed the baton to His disciples on the Day of Pentecost and they had tongues of fire over their heads and they spoke in a way everyone could understand them in their own native tongue. Acts 2 says:

> [1]When the day of Pentecost came, they were all together in one place. [2]Suddenly a sound like the blowing of a violent wind came from heaven and filled the whole house where they were sitting. [3]They saw what seemed to be tongues of fire that separated and came to rest on each of them. [4]All of them were filled with the Holy Spirit and began to speak in other tongues[a] as the Spirit enabled them.

> [5]Now there were staying in Jerusalem God-fearing Jews from every nation under heaven. [6]When they heard this sound, a crowd came together in bewilderment, because each one heard them speaking in his own language. [7]Utterly amazed, they asked: "Are not all these men who are speaking Galileans? [8]Then how is it that each of us hears them in his own native language? [9]Parthians, Medes and Elamites; residents of Mesopotamia, Judea and Cappadocia, Pontus and Asia, [10]Phrygia and Pamphylia, Egypt and the parts of Libya near Cyrene; visitors from Rome [11] (both Jews and converts to Judaism); Cretans and Arabs-we hear them declaring the wonders of God in our own tongues!" [12]Amazed and perplexed, they asked one another, "What does this mean?"

> [13]Some, however, made fun of them and said, "They have had too much wine.[b]"

In the next chapter, Peter is healing the crippled beggar. By chapter 5, we are told:

The apostles performed many miraculous signs and wonders among the people. And all the believers used to meet together in

Solomon's Colonnade. [13]No one else dared join them, even though they were highly regarded by the people. [14]Nevertheless, more and more men and women believed in the Lord and were added to their number. [15]As a result, people brought the sick into the streets and laid them on beds and mats so that at least Peter's shadow might fall on some of them as he passed by. [16]Crowds gathered also from the towns around Jerusalem, bringing their sick and those tormented by evil[a] spirits, and all of them were healed.

God has demonstrated miracles throughout the rest of the New Testament. Regretfully, many have embraced the ideology that miracles ceased when the apostles died out. That is sad. There are many ministers of the gospel who believe in answered prayers but deny miracles ever really occur. Some say, they have never witnessed a miracle from God. To those, I encourage them to read Matthew 17:19-21.

> [19]Then the disciples came to Jesus in private and asked, "Why couldn't we drive it out?"
>
> [20]He replied, "Because you have so little faith. I tell you the truth, if you have faith as small as a mustard seed, you can say to this mountain, 'Move from here to there' and it will move. Nothing will be impossible for you."[a]

That says a great deal about the strength of man's faith through the generations. Like many today, I bought into the philosophy that had been taught in generations prior. Then I went to Bible College and saw the discrepancies between what many Christians had embraced as truth and what potential actually existed with miraculous healing.

Again, many have placed their god in a box throughout the week only to take him out to worship him once a week. God started stirring in my heart and I began pursuing God as He had wanted me to do for decades. It has been exciting and totally out of this world to experience my faith rather than just claiming a faith of my parents by simply going through the motions.

Many have limited the awesomeness of God and have limited His existence to this god who spun this universe into motion and then checked out. We have had to attempt to manage life as we know it on our own. That is so far from the truth! Every time there is a catastrophe, it is our Maker's attempt to call us back to humility before Him. Desperation brings us to humility more quickly than our gaudiness and pride ever will.

God has said in Hebrews 13:5-6,

> "Never will I leave you;
> never will I forsake you."[a] [6]So we say with confidence,
> "The Lord is my helper; I will not be afraid.
> What can man do to me?"[b]

Even King David, a man after God's own heart, entrusted Himself completely in the hands of God. David truly embraced the dance with God when he stood before Goliath. Consider I Samuel 17:

> [32] David said to Saul, "Let no one lose heart on account of this Philistine; your servant will go and fight him."

> [33] Saul replied, "You are not able to go out against this Philistine and fight him; you are only a boy, and he has been a fighting man from his youth."

> [34] But David said to Saul, "Your servant has been keeping his father's sheep. When a lion or a bear came and carried off a sheep from the flock, [35] I went after it, struck it and rescued the sheep from its mouth. When it turned on me, I seized it by its hair, struck it and killed it. [36] Your servant has killed both the lion and the bear; **this uncircumcised Philistine will be like one of them, because he has defied the armies of the living God. [37] The LORD who delivered me from the paw of the lion and the paw of the bear will deliver me from the hand of this Philistine."**
> Saul said to David, "Go, and the LORD be with you."

> [38] Then Saul dressed David in his own tunic. He put a coat of armor on him and a bronze helmet on his head. [39] David fastened on his sword over the tunic and tried walking around, because he was not used to them.
> "I cannot go in these," he said to Saul, "because I am not used to them." So he took them off. [40] Then he took his staff in his hand, chose five smooth stones from the stream, put them in the pouch of his shepherd's bag and, with his sling in his hand, approached the Philistine.

[41] Meanwhile, the Philistine, with his shield bearer in front of him, kept coming closer to David. [42] He looked David over and saw that he was only a boy, ruddy and handsome, and he despised him. [43] He said to David, "Am I a dog, that you come at me with sticks?" And the Philistine cursed David by his gods. [44] "Come here," he said, "and I'll give your flesh to the birds of the air and the beasts of the field!"

[45] David said to the Philistine, "You come against me with sword and spear and javelin, but I come against you in the name of the LORD Almighty, the God of the armies of Israel, whom you have defied. [46] This day the LORD will hand you over to me, and I'll strike you down and cut off your head. Today I will give the carcasses of the Philistine army to the birds of the air and the beasts of the earth, and the whole world will know that there is a God in Israel. [47] All those gathered here will know that it is not by sword or spear that the LORD saves; for the battle is the LORD's, and he will give all of you into our hands."

When David embraced the dance with God, God gave him a spiritual and military victory. David was truly a man after God's own heart; and in God's timing, God placed him on the throne as the second king of Israel. David penned many of the Psalms during his reign as king. Many have been able to recite the 23rd Psalm by heart at a very early age. Many use it as a comfort when a friend or relative has passed. For those not familiar with it, David wrote:

[1] The LORD is my shepherd, I shall not be in want.

[2] He makes me lie down in green pastures,
   he leads me beside quiet waters,

[3] he restores my soul.
   He guides me in paths of righteousness
   for his name's sake.

[4] Even though I walk
   through the valley of the shadow of death, [a]
   I will fear no evil,
   for you are with me;
   your rod and your staff,
   they comfort me.

⁵ You prepare a table before me
>   in the presence of my enemies.
>   You anoint my head with oil;
>   my cup overflows.

⁶ Surely goodness and love will follow me
>   all the days of my life,
>   and I will dwell in the house of the LORD
>   forever.

After David had become king of Israel, he had too much time on his hands when he sent his soldiers out to fight without him. David had had many victories and he was certain the army would be able to manage without him. Satan smelled blood. David went up on the roof top of his castle. He was bored and as he looked over the edge of the castle, David saw a beautiful woman bathing at a distance. Satan filled David's heart with lust and passion for this beautiful young woman in a sensuous context. He ordered his servant to go bring her to him and he did.

David, previously a man after God's own heart, embraced his dance with the devil. Satan approached him in a sensuous way. Satan ensnared his hooks of evil into the flesh of David with passion. David embraced it without thought or any consideration for possible ramifications, even though he **knew** it was a sin against the God he served. Yet willfully, David committed adultery regardless. Days later the king was approached and informed that Bathsheba was with child. She had conceived while her husband Uriah was out on the battlefield. How was he going to cover his tracks?

Well of first order; send for Uriah to return to the king to update the king on the progress of the war efforts. Of course, that was all a ploy to get Uriah home with his wife Bathsheba so they could make love that night before returning to battle.

II Samuel 11 says:

⁹ But Uriah slept at the entrance to the palace with all his master's servants and did not go down to his house.

¹⁰ When David was told, "Uriah did not go home," he asked him, "Haven't you just come from a distance? Why didn't you go home?" (Strike one!)

¹¹ Uriah said to David, "The ark and Israel and Judah are staying in tents, and my master Joab and my lord's men are camped in the open fields. How could I go to my house to eat and drink and lie with my wife? As surely as you live, I will not do such a thing!"

¹² Then David said to him, "Stay here one more day, and tomorrow I will send you back." So Uriah remained in Jerusalem that day and the next. ¹³ At David's invitation, he ate and drank with him, and David made him drunk. But in the evening Uriah went out to sleep on his mat among his master's servants; he did not go home. (Strike two!)

¹⁴ In the morning David wrote a letter to Joab and sent it with Uriah. ¹⁵ In it he wrote, "Put Uriah in the front line where the fighting is fiercest. Then withdraw from him so he will be struck down and die."

¹⁶ So while Joab had the city under siege, he put Uriah at a place where he knew the strongest defenders were. ¹⁷ When the men of the city came out and fought against Joab, some of the men in David's army fell; moreover, Uriah the Hittite died. (Strike three! .... God removed Himself from David because there was sin in the camp.)

Now, not only had David committed adultery, now he was additionally a murderer. A chapter later, God sent His servant Nathan to call King David to task. After using the parable of the man who had many sheep verses the man, who had only one ewe lamb,

⁵ David burned with anger against the man and said to Nathan, "As surely as the LORD lives, the man who did this deserves to die! ⁶ He must pay for that lamb four times over, because he did such a thing and had no pity."

⁷ Then Nathan said to David, "**You are the man!** This is what the LORD, the God of Israel, says: 'I anointed you king over Israel, and I delivered you from the hand of Saul. ⁸ I gave your master's house to you, and your master's wives into your arms. I gave you the house of Israel and Judah. And if all this had been too little, I would have given you even more. ⁹ Why did you despise the word of the LORD by doing what is evil in his eyes? You struck down Uriah the Hittite with the sword and took his wife to be your

own. You killed him with the sword of the Ammonites. [10] Now, therefore, the sword will never depart from your house, because you despised me and took the wife of Uriah the Hittite to be your own.'

[11] "This is what the LORD says: 'Out of your own household I am going to bring calamity upon you. Before your very eyes I will take your wives and give them to one who is close to you, and he will lie with your wives in broad daylight. [12] You did it in secret, but I will do this thing in broad daylight before all Israel.' "

[13] Then David said to Nathan, "I have sinned against the LORD."

Nathan replied, **"The LORD has taken away your sin. You are not going to die. [14] But because by doing this you have made the enemies of the LORD show utter contempt, [a] the son born to you will die."**

[15] After Nathan had gone home, the LORD struck the child that Uriah's wife had borne to David, and he became ill.

The Lord finally claimed the life of David's son, even though he had fasted. And there was strife in his household the rest of his adult life, because he never pondered the possible ramifications from the sins he willfully committed. Oh, the webs we weave when we embrace the dance with sin.

God restored David to his throne and God was with him. Nevertheless, David lived his life for his Creator when justice was served for every sin he had embraced. Under the old dispensation of the law, all of Israel had embraced the eye for an eye and a tooth for a tooth mindset prior to the Ultimate Sacrifice that introduced grace a millennium later.

In the New Testament the best demonstration of embracing the dance with restoration was demonstrated by the Apostle Peter. Go back to the upper room encounter prior to the arrest of Jesus prior to His crucifixion. The story picks up in Matthew 26, beginning with verses 32:

[31]Then Jesus told them, "This very night you will all fall away on account of me, for it is written:

" 'I will strike the shepherd,
    and the sheep of the flock will be scattered.'[c] [32]But after I have risen, I will go ahead of you into Galilee."

³³Peter replied, "Even if all fall away on account of you, I never will."

³⁴"I tell you the truth," Jesus answered, "this very night, before the rooster crows, you will disown me three times."

³⁵But Peter declared, "Even if I have to die with you, I will never disown you." And all the other disciples said the same.

But then the test came. Jesus was arrested. And in the midst of Jesus being tried, Peter was questioned three times in the same chapter.

⁶⁹Now Peter was sitting out in the courtyard, and a servant girl came to him. "You also were with Jesus of Galilee," she said.

⁷⁰But he denied it before them all. "I don't know what you're talking about," he said.

⁷¹Then he went out to the gateway, where another girl saw him and said to the people there, "This fellow was with Jesus of Nazareth."

⁷²He denied it again, with an oath: "I don't know the man!"

⁷³After a little while, those standing there went up to Peter and said, "Surely you are one of them, for your accent gives you away."

⁷⁴Then he began to call down curses on himself and he swore to them, "I don't know the man!"

Immediately a rooster crowed. ⁷⁵Then Peter remembered the word Jesus had spoken: "Before the rooster crows, you will disown me three times." And he went outside and wept bitterly.

Even though Peter had committed to serving Christ to the point of death, Jesus already foreknew that Peter would be put on the spot and deny he ever knew Jesus three times before the cock crowed. It came into fruition just as Jesus had said and Peter wept bitterly.

Fast forward beyond the crucifixion and the resurrection of Jesus Christ. The disciples had returned to their trade of fishing when Jesus appeared again in John 21. Peter couldn't forgive himself. He had been given opportunity and he failed. But before His ascension, Jesus knew Peter had to embrace the dance with restoration. Notice the details with Peter when Jesus met them for the third time following His resurrection.

> ¹¹Simon Peter climbed aboard and dragged the net ashore. It was full of large fish, 153, but even with so many the net was not torn. ¹²Jesus said to them, "Come and have breakfast." None of the disciples dared ask him, "Who are you?" They knew it was the Lord. ¹³Jesus came, took the bread and gave it to them, and did the same with the fish. ¹⁴This was now the third time Jesus appeared to his disciples after he was raised from the dead.

> ¹⁵When they had finished eating, Jesus said to Simon Peter, "Simon son of John, do you truly love me more than these?"
> "Yes, Lord," he said, "you know that I love you."
> Jesus said, "Feed my lambs."

> ¹⁶Again Jesus said, "Simon son of John, do you truly love me?"
> He answered, "Yes, Lord, you know that I love you."
> Jesus said, "Take care of my sheep."

> ¹⁷ The third time he said to him, "Simon son of John, do you love me?"
> Peter was hurt because Jesus asked him the third time, "Do you love me?" He said, "Lord, you know all things; you know that I love you."

> Jesus said, "Feed my sheep. ¹⁸ I tell you the truth, when you were younger you dressed yourself and went where you wanted; but when you are old you will stretch out your hands, and someone else will dress you and lead you where you do not want to go." ¹⁹Jesus said this to indicate the kind of death by which Peter would glorify God. Then he said to him, "Follow me!"

Jesus knew Peter was pretty bummed when he didn't remain true to his word and denied he even knew Jesus. But Jesus also knew Peter, the rock, was going to be one of His most powerful spokesmen on the Day of Pentecost and following. So Jesus knew Peter needed grace and restoration prior to his call to ministry.

I always thought it was imperative Jesus paralleled the three times Peter denied he ever knew Jesus with the three times Jesus asked, "Peter, do you love Me?" "Yes, Peter, you messed up just as I said you would. But do you really love Me?" You see, Jesus knew what was yet to come following Pentecost. And He also knew Peter had to be restored and strengthened prior to the event.

Because Peter embraced the dance of restoration, Peter rocked the world as he knew it on the Day of Pentecost and after. Thousands were saved because he had taken the leap of faith to total restoration with his Creator.

Every one of us has the opportunity to embrace the dance with total restoration with God every day. Regretfully, few embrace the dance and many are flooded with guilt and the enemy holds them hostage there to prevent them from becoming the person God wants them to become. I have had many come to my office for counseling who identify themselves as unforgivable. The choices they had made prior, had sealed their fate for life. But when I get them to a clearer understanding of God's grace, they truly take that leap of faith. God embraces them and totally rocks their world to a clearer understanding of His purpose.

Consider the story of Kim. Kim had been brought up in an upbringing without God or church. In fact, Kim had never experienced the love from her parents as God intended. Life initially was hard for Kim. Kim always had a longing to love and to be loved, but she never really knew what love really was. She had never really experienced it. Desperate for love, she was looking for love in all of the wrong places. She went carousing and bar hopping just to fill the deep void that existed in her heart emotionally.

Kim went through two hard marriages. In her first marriage, she embraced a drunk and a verbal abuser that scared her into submission. He was definitely secular in his thinking and actions. Carousing was routine. Two kids later, Kim knew she could no longer keep her children subject to the abuse and poor atmosphere. She finally mustard up the courage to leave the sick dynamic that she had previously embraced.

Rather than turning to a God she had never heard of prior, she again embraced the dance with a liar and a womanizer. He had multiple affairs on her and yet denied it to her face. She embraced the dance with the devil. He persuaded her to resort to elevated anxiety and panic attacks. That dictated her responses to the suspicions of her husband's drug paraphernalia and carousing with other women. She embraced the lies he told her.

By the time she entered my office, she had accepted Christ as her Savior; but she had yet to experience Christ and her faith. Her words she said in the first therapy session still resound through my memory to this day. She said, "I'm beyond fixing! I have made so many poor choices in life, **I can't be fixed**!" Her anxiety level was a twelve of ten and her depression was a seven of ten.

Over time, I encouraged Kim to take a leap of faith and embrace the dance of restoration with her Savior. Desperate after attempting life on her own terms multiple times, she finally took that leap of faith and Jesus restored her in a powerful way. I have encouraged Kim to share her story with you after she took that leap of faith.

> *" I can still remember mom's harsh words; "You hate your sister Kay, you always stepped on her fingers when she was crawling." I couldn't have been over two or three years old, as I am two years older than Kay. I didn't understand, I didn't hate Kay either. I also remember my older sister Karen beating me up all the time and mom being mad at me and it always involved Kay. I was always in trouble because of Kay.*
>
> *When I was sixteen years old, I got a part time job and worked to support myself and to help mom and dad out. Kay would steal all my clothes, perfume, shoes etc. that I bought and tell mom that her boyfriend bought them for her. Mom believed her and made me let Kay have my things. When Kay got married, she laid everything she had stolen on my bed and said I could have them back. I went and got mom and showed her the truth but mom never said a word. Not "I'm sorry Kim," nothing.*
>
> *We were taught good morals, (don't lie, cheat, steal, etc.) but we were not brought up in a Godly home. Mom and dad never told us one time that they loved us and rarely got hugs much less kisses. I remember when Kay and her husband moved to Florida, that is when mom and dad started to tell us, "I love you." I was twenty-six or twenty-seven years old.*

I was starved for love and affection as a child growing up but never got it. My dad was very verbally overbearing and I can remember being scared to death when he would beller at us. One time, I dropped mom's good ink pen between the washer and the dryer. She said that when dad got home from work he would move the dryer and get it. I was devastated! I was so afraid of him, I just shook and was sick inside, wishing mom or I could retrieve the pen ourselves. I also can remember going to Girl Scout camp for a week. When it was over, I definitely didn't want go home.

Jodi was in my Girl Scout troop. We really hit it off as friends. Her mother was our leader. I really loved Jodi, she was a great friend. I must of went home and told mom about me and Jodi and mom said, "You can't be friends with Jodi her dad owns the local paper." I was devastated, I believed mom and backed away from Jodi, and only had dysfunctional friends from then on.

When I was eighteen, I became pregnant. I had friends that were having sex so I thought I'd try it. I haven't seen the father of the child since I told him I was pregnant at three months.

While I was pregnant, I met Danny. It was very hard for me to tell him and my father I was pregnant. I just wanted to die. Mom and dad didn't kick me out but they reminded me of my mistake often. Danny accepted me also. Danny and I had sex. My dad even told him to go ahead; that he couldn't hurt me any.

My daughter was born and Danny and I were married four months later. Things seemed really good in the beginning but only after a few months Danny started going out and staying out all weekend. He would also leave in the middle of the night while I was asleep. Of course he would lie to me and I would embrace his lies, and accept him back. This went on our whole twelve years of marriage. Seven years into our marriage we had a son, I had always so desperately wanted to give Danny a child because of how he accepted and adopted and loved my daughter. But he continued to drink and be gone all weekend. When he would come home we would fight horribly until I gave in and believed his lies. We would go back to life as we knew it, until the next time and then it would be hell all over again. We were always broke and couldn't pay the bills, couldn't buy groceries half the time. He would always rant and rave at me that it was my fault.

The next three years I spent drinking, carousing and going to bars all the time. I wanted to see what was so great about bar hopping as Danny had done. I was definitely at one of my lowest levels.

I met David in a bar. He was nice, bought me a drink with no strings attached. He was nice to me, we drank a lot and did a few drugs. He told me, "I just wanted a burnt out divorced woman with a couple of kids that I can love and be good to." I fell for it hook, line and sinker. It wasn't long till he would be so messed up that he would pass out at my son's baseball games, make a fool of himself at my daughter's football games; pee his pants anywhere, set the bed on fire twice with his smoking and drinking and also the bathroom floor. It didn't take me long to realize the mistake I made in marrying him but now I was also pregnant. We had a son and I knew David wouldn't be any help at all. I decided I would have to quit drinking and partying with him as someone needed to be responsible for the baby and my other two children as well. I would not divorce him because the courts could give joint custody. If not that he would have visitation rights every other weekend and possibly the summer too.

The divorce from Danny was so bad he would end up marrying the town drunk and whore which made my kids life hell. Her dad who was sixty eight years old was even stalking my sixteen year old daughter. I went to the law, a lawyer and the welfare to only find out that Danny's dad had bought them off. I was on my own.

Between David being a drunk, liar, womanizer and a druggie I couldn't bear the thought of him having complete control over our son while I wasn't around; teaching our son all of his bad habits. Let alone our son being around his lying and very dysfunctional family. So I stayed with David and accepted his crap. He made passes at two women and was chasing after a woman he worked with. The women he worked with would just sing his praises. He would go out of his way to help them get caught up, lift heavy boxes for them.

While at home, I would come in with four or five heavy have hampers of laundry; ten or twelve bags of groceries and four or five 50lb bags of salt for the water conditioner. Not to mention a 50 lb bag of dog food, while he was laying on the couch watching TV, while I was carrying everything in by myself. Finally, I couldn't take it anymore and filed for divorce.

Right after our son graduated from high school and went to college, David came home from work one morning so drugged out, I watched him try to open a can of soup for half an hour. He didn't know where he was, who he was, who I was or nothing. The light came on in my head that this was enough. I called the police; they called an ambulance to take him to the hospital. I had enough.

Right after our son was born, I knew I couldn't raise my kids without God. We found a good church and the kids and I attended regularly. The kids and I were baptized but I still didn't know what it was to have a personal relationship with Jesus. I still knew nothing about spiritual warfare. As a result, my life just kept going in a downward spiral.

Three months before David came home all drugged out, I knew something was going on with him. He was acting weird, something was wrong. I tried relentlessly to catch him and figure out what was going on but to no avail. I would drive out to his work and would just drive myself crazy trying to find out what was going on. Then one day I was watching

TV and thought of something I wanted to tell him. So I went up to the bedroom to tell him and there he was rolling a big fat joint, you talk about Divine Intervention! How sweet! The Lord showed up when I didn't even expect it! Well we have been having major problems every since. I do believe there was a woman involved too. To make it even harder on my emotional stress, David decided to go to church and get baptized. I really believed he was into it (and maybe he was), but the lies and deception continued.

We are separated, going through an ugly divorce and I can't take the emotional pain any longer so I started going to John for help! I told him, "I am so messed up, I am beyond fixing." John definitely had his work cut out for him.

I kept going to John and also left my home church and started going to his church he was pastoring. In Sunday school they were doing a study on R-12 a Chip Ingram series. Between the R-12 series and John's counseling, were my eyes opened?! John would tell me; "Kim you have to let go of the rope; let go and let God." And WOW when I did, it was awesome. But you also have to remember Satan will come along enticing you to grab that rope again, (which I have several times), but every time I've fallen, Jesus was right there to pick me up again.

I've been going to church for 21 years and I've heard preachers say, "You have to have a personal relationship with Jesus," But that was about it, they didn't follow up with how to do that or offer any help how to do that. Through John and Chip I've learned how. I was so excited to learn that it's not about me, it's about Jesus! Also it's not about what you do like tithing, sitting through church every week, helping people (which are all good things Christians do), but what Jesus really wants is you; all of you. Inside and out! He wants you to give your whole self and everything you have to Him; (your kids, husband, wife, car, house, job, grandkids, finances, health; all of you and what's yours) and He wants you to seek Him and read His Word every day, and Wow!

When you do, it is the greatest experience ever. You can feel His presence and He also talks with you!!

John kept telling me "Wait till you dance with Jesus!" I have several times. He's there; He's with you! It's beyond words! How awesome it is! You can't stop laughing, enjoying yourself; you just throw your head back and you are in for the greatest experience of your life! You know He is with you; you can feel Him and His awesome love! He assures you, "I am with you always." But you have to be careful, because Satan will be looking for opportunities to bring you back down; I just tell him, "In the name of Jesus, get away from me." And it works! Then just keep clinging to Jesus and don't let go of Him. Pray to Him, Praise Him, talk with Him and read His Word!

I have found that spending an hour or two in God's Word every morning, and praising Him and talking to Him every chance I get every day keeps me close to Him. When I don't, I'm in trouble because Satan will use the opportunity to start his doubts and lies with me. But don't despair; every time I've come back to Jesus, He forgives me and He's there for me again. He's never really left me, I've left Him.

You know I always was afraid of God (maybe because I was afraid of my dad?) and I always thought I wasn't good enough, but look at the Bible people; they were just ordinary people like us. They had their problems too. God has shown me that He can use people just like me and a lot of times He uses broken people because they've been there. They know from experience how it feels!

So let go and let God! He longs to restore you to a beautiful lasting relationship with you! Yes You! There are also great books out there like this one of John's that God has inspired that will help you also. Every day, just talk to Him. Walk with Him. Learn all you can about Him. Give Him everything that is yours. And watch the mountains He will move for you!

God is AWESOME!

I also wanted to share with you that all along I thought David had a girlfriend. I've tried to catch him to no avail for almost 3 years. I was an emotional wreck to say the least! I was at my granddaughter's baseball game when low and behold, here came David. He drove right by us and stopped across the street at his girlfriend's house!! He didn't even see us! You talk about Divine Intervention!

Through my restoration process, God has made many revelations to me; especially that Danny was cheating on me with multiple women including two that I stood next to at work for 32 years. That Kay was always telling mom lies on me and I learned at a very early age to accept lies and believe that I was this bad lying little girl who didn't deserve anything good in life. So see why I always believed my husband's lies? I thank God and praise Him for showing me the truth! Jesus is the truth as He was truly God with us.

God longs to restore you to His calling once again. Until you are willing to take that leap of faith, you are limiting what God can and will do through you. It is imperative for every genuine Christian to embrace the dance of restoration with their Creator.

1. What does Matthew 17:19-21 tell us about our faith or lack of? What does that say about the faith of most churches?

2. Discuss God's ongoing miracles throughout history. What have each in your group been taught regarding miracles? In light of scripture, was your previous understanding skewed or accurate?

3. What has led so many to believe that if there is a God, he has checked out and left us to survive on our own? What are the discrepancies of that belief?

4. What has prevented people from pursuing God daily? How has the devil lured God's creation from God to limit their faith and power?

5. As stated in Hebrews 13:5-6, God promises he will never leave nor forsake us. Yet there are times it seems like God is so far away. How can this be aside from the poor choices we have made ourselves to leave God out of our daily lives? How Can we get back on track in our spiritual walk with God?

6. Why is it we can talk about the faith of King David before Goliath and we cheer on David's faith, yet we so easily discredit the possibility of us having the same experiences of faith with the God we worship?

7. How did the adversary trip up the man after God's own heart? How did he lure David away from God? How does he lure people away from God today?

8. How had David developed an attitude of entitlement? How should that caution us to utilize humility rather than the attitude of entitlement? How should we respond to beauty and glamour when it crosses our path?

9. When David strayed from God and Bathsheba had reported her pregnancy, what was David's immediate response? Why? How did his response lead him into more sinfulness? How could the truth have set him free?

10. How was David convicted? What did God require of David prior to forgiveness and restoration? How does that parallel with our Christian walk?

11. Has guilt from your past limited you ability to fully embrace total restoration to God's purpose in your life? How do you personally interpret Psalm 103:11-13?

12. Understanding we serve a limitless God, how can spiritual restoration impact you personally as well as the people around you? How could God place you on the dream team of his purpose?

Embracing the Dance of True Intimacy with God

Dancing in true intimacy with God is not something to take lightly. Deuteronomy 6 says:

> ²³ But he brought us out from there to bring us in and give us the land that he promised on oath to our forefathers. ²⁴ The LORD commanded us to obey all these decrees and to **fear the LORD our God, so that we might always prosper and be kept alive, as is the case today.** ²⁵ **And if we are careful to obey all this law before the LORD our God, as he has commanded us, that will be our righteousness."**

For those who have never experienced their faith, perhaps the following comparison will gain you perspective. I was raised before Dr. Spock ever removed corporal punishment from our culture. Both of my parents embraced Proverbs 13 when it came to discipline in the house I grew up in. Proverbs 13 says:

> ²⁴ He who spares the rod hates his son,
>   but he who loves him is careful to discipline him.

> ²⁵ The righteous eat to their hearts' content,
>   but the stomach of the wicked goes hungry.

When my sisters or I crossed the line of our parents, they embraced the dance of discipline. If the hand on the derriere wasn't persuasive enough, wooden spoons were always a healthy second.

During my seventh grade year as defined earlier in the book, the pharmacological change had made me belligerent and defiant to my parents. I know that is hard for some of my readers to believe but I was the "strong willed child" in our household and it got me in trouble a lot that year. I am grateful God gave me a dad who stepped up to the plate for this strong willed child he had to raise.

At age twelve I was right on cue when it came to the rebellious phase of redefining who I was. I struggled with that transition from child to adolescent and then adolescent to adulthood. I rebelled against both of my parents in many ways. As I reflect back over time, that was a phase in my life I have little desire to return to but I embraced it nonetheless.

Dad stepped up to be the dad God had called him to be. He found the currency that broke my rebellious spirit. Spanking no longer worked. There wasn't a pain I couldn't handle or so I thought. Finally my dad assured me either my rebellious spirit or my back would be broken first. Those were my options. Every time I mouthed off to them as a defiant thirteen year old, I was escorted to the garage where I was instructed to get the hand held auger used to hand dig post holes. He would then escort me to the edge of the field and point at where he wanted a posthole dug. He would wander off to work on the farm equipment with his promise of return to a hole that had better be completed on his return. He watched me from a distance and when the posthole digger was practically buried in the hole he would come out and ask if I had cooled my jets yet. I would spout off again and he'd kick the dirt back in the hole, point to another spot saying he wanted another hole dug where he specified.

As I was digging the second posthole, I recalled the words of my older sister Carol, when she said, "You know you could save yourself from a backache if you would learn to shut your mouth." That battle was always fought normally by the second posthole. "Submit and shut up with apology? ………. Or Back ache?" And even though it tasted like vinegar coming out, I apologized nonetheless. One phrase that has played again and again in my head was the line dad instilled in me at a very early age. He always said, "Throughout life, you will either choose to use your back or you will choose to use your head."

He always stated he personally chose to use his head rather than his back. It was less painful. And he was right. (I learned to have a healthy fear and respect of my dad and we have been best friends ever since.) Had he not mandated discipline at the early age of 12, I never would have been able to embrace the only commandment with a promise.

Exodus 20:12 says:

¹² "Honor your father and your mother, **so that you may live long in the land the LORD your God is giving you.**

That was a promise worth embracing and I have always had a healthy respect and fear of my earthly father ever since. That is the healthy fear and respect we need for our Heavenly Father as well. As discussed in the chapter earlier God demands total submission to His will. When we experience our genuine faith in Him and continually come to Him with a confessing and repentant heart, He will initiate His intimate dance with us.

I was back at our home church at Plum Creek, following the lobectomy and removal of the damaged portion of my brain. When it came to prayer time with praises and concerns, I walked before the church family, who had followed my surgery intently. I praised God for pulling me through the surgery unscathed. I told them about the prayer encounter prior to the surgery and said, "I am excited about serving God and experiencing my faith in whatever direction He calls us to. I can't wait to find out where He wants to use us the most." And God has miraculously moved mountains in our lives ever since. Like Paul we have learned what it is like to have plenty; what it is like to be in want. Like Elijah, we have had the raven experience. In I Kings 17, take note of how God cared for His own.

Then the word of the LORD came to Elijah: ³ "Leave here, turn eastward and hide in the Kerith Ravine, east of the Jordan. ⁴ You will drink from the brook, and I have ordered the ravens to feed you there."

⁵ So he did what the LORD had told him. He went to the Kerith Ravine, east of the Jordan, and stayed there. ⁶ The ravens brought him bread and meat in the morning and bread and meat in the evening, and he drank from the brook.

God has come through every time there has been a need in our family. Every time bills were due but there were more bills than there was income, God has miraculously sent unexpected money from churches who we have worked with in times prior. When foods were scarce, church members and family would willfully give us staples that were surplus in their cabinets.

Experiencing an intimate dance with God, is an awesome thing. I cannot describe it with words to give it justice. By the grace of God I was able to intimately embrace the dances with my Maker. I have been given revelation after revelation about God and His relationship with His church and His longing for true Christians to experience their faith. He wants us to go the distance with Him. He wants us to talk the talk but He additionally wants us to embrace the spiritual walk with Him.

In the Garden of Eden, God walked with Adam and Eve in the cool of the day every day. Prior to the fall, He walked with His creation every day because He was in love with His perfect Creation. He wanted His creation to embrace the dance of intimacy with Him every day. Adam and Eve had 24/7 access to infinite wisdom as long as they embraced the intimate dance with their Maker. Can't you imagine the answered questions Adam and Eve must have asked? God enjoyed the intimate relationship with what He had created in His own image. It is likely He embraced it every day because He already foreknew the fall would happen and He would be separated from them for a season once they fell.

Prior to Chip Ingram's authoring R12, I had already been using the love triangle with God in the therapeutic setting. With his permission, I would like to offer a final phase God wants us to embrace when we truly accept His invitation to intimately embrace the dance with our Creator upon His invitation.

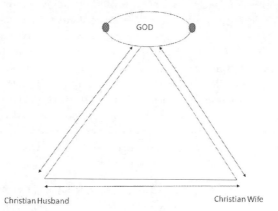

God longs for all of us to return to His Garden of Eden intimacy with Him again. But God said there is only one way to the Garden to intimately accept the dance with Him. Jesus said, "I am the way the truth and the life. No man comes to the Father but **through** Me." Jesus went through the entire "I Am" series to affirm He was and is the only bridge back to the Garden of Eden experience with our Creator. That is why salvation through Christ is so important to be witnessed by all of God's creation.

God doesn't really want us to stay in the love triangle formation in our relationship to Him. God wants us to be so intimately His that the triangle is no longer necessary to stay in fellowship with us. God wants us to orbit around His very will of being what He calls us to, to fulfill His purpose. When we take it to the level of orbiting around God and his purpose, harmony is restored in marriages, households, cities, churches and nations. We are His workmanship. Now, read Ephesians 2 and see if this gives you knew insight and perspective of who He has called us to be.

> [1]As for you, you were dead in your transgressions and sins, [2]in which you used to live when you followed the ways of this world and of the ruler of the kingdom of the air, the spirit who is now at work in those who are disobedient. [3]All of us also lived among them at one time, gratifying the cravings of our sinful nature[a] and following its desires and thoughts. Like the rest, we were by

nature objects of wrath. [4]But because of his great love for us, God, who is rich in mercy, [5]made us alive with Christ even when we were dead in transgressions—it is by grace you have been saved. [6]And God raised us up with Christ and seated us with him in the heavenly realms in Christ Jesus, [7]in order that in the coming ages he might show the incomparable riches of his grace, expressed in his kindness to us in Christ Jesus. [8]For it is by grace you have been saved, through faith—and this not from yourselves, it is the gift of God— [9]not by works, so that no one can boast. [10]For we are God's workmanship, created in Christ Jesus to do good works, which God prepared in advance for us to do.

[11]Therefore, remember that formerly you who are Gentiles by birth and called "uncircumcised" by those who call themselves "the circumcision" (that done in the body by the hands of men)— [12]remember that at that time you were separate from Christ, excluded from citizenship in Israel and foreigners to the covenants of the promise, without hope and without God in the world. [13]But now in Christ Jesus you who once were far away have been brought near through the blood of Christ.

[14]For he himself is our peace, who has made the two one and has destroyed the barrier, the dividing wall of hostility, [15]by abolishing in his flesh the law with its commandments and regulations. His purpose was to create in himself one new man out of the two, thus making peace, [16]and in this one body to reconcile both of them to God **through the cross**, by which he put to death their hostility. [17]He came and preached peace to you who were far away and peace to those who were near. [18]For **through him** we both have access to the Father by one Spirit.

[19]Consequently, you are no longer foreigners and aliens, but fellow citizens with God's people and members of God's household, [20]built on the foundation of the apostles and prophets, with Christ Jesus himself as the chief cornerstone. [21]In him the whole building is joined together and rises to become a holy temple in the Lord. [22]And in him you too are being built together to become a dwelling in which God lives by his Spirit.

In concluding this chapter, I am certain there are many skeptics who even call themselves Christians; people who have talked the talk but have never taken the step of faith, embracing their faith in the arms of Jesus. And there are probably some agnostics or atheist who would easily conclude this author is really out there and it would be easy to walk away and never experience nor embrace the dance with our Creator as He so longs for us to do. Now is your opportunity to prove me wrong.

If you can take a child like faith, surrender **EVERYTHING** you have to God with a repentant heart, seek transformation at His will and be baptized as the Great Commission calls us to do, I guarantee you, you will finally embrace the dance of intimacy with your Creator. It is literally out of this world!!!!!!!

Miracles happen every day throughout God's creation. Let's go back to the analogy of the caterpillar. Many of you reading this book have already embraced the struggle of what you believe spiritually. If I were watching the struggle and willfully went to open the cocoon for you to free you from the struggle, you would never have the strength in your wings to fly. I encourage you to embrace the struggle on your own. God will send the right person at the right time to say the right thing that will persuade you through the struggle to give you the fortitude and strength you will need to break free from being held hostage by a dead belief system of various religions and faiths. God longs to assist you in the heart transplant you will encounter should you take this leap of faith. I dare you! And I pray that God will totally rock your world to His Glory and Majesty.

"Thank you God for revealing Yourself so intimately to me when I finally took that leap of faith in Your arms. Lord, please remove the blinders from the readers who have never truly witnessed nor experienced their faith in the intimate relationship and dance with You, as you have so longed for us to do."

1. Why are we to have a healthy fear of God when he wants us to dance with him in true intimacy? Isn't that a paradox? Why?

2. Why is a healthy fear of God so critical? How can a healthy fear of God spawn truer intimacy with the will of God?

3. Did Lucifer have a healthy fear of God? What resulted?

4. Why is the one commandment regarding respect for parents the only commandment with a promise? How does that parallel with our need of a healthy fear of God's sovereignty?

5. What has resulted in our culture, since the removal of corporal punishment? What adjectives describe the youth of our culture today? How does in differ from 20-30 years ago?

6. With the skewed understanding of biblical corporal punishment, how has that affected our intimate relationship with God? What can we do restore the possibility of intimacy with God?

7. God has longed for all of us to return to the Garden of Eden experience with true spiritual intimacy toward him. How can we now obtain that same type of intimacy with God in this sin-sick world?

8. What is the only way to obtain that type of relationship with God in our culture today? Why is there only one way? How does that synchronize with Jesus illustration in Matthew 7:13-14?

9. Why does God want us to orbit around him and his will for our lives?

10. How does our total alignment with God's will restore harmony in relationships, households and nations? Explain.

11. What is Paul's perspective in his writing of Ephesians 2?

12. Many who are reading this material feel spiritually paralyzed at best. How can you return to the child like faith God has called you to?

Embracing the Dance with Broken Chains

Many who have tried to face challenges in life have often times attempted to mask their pains in life with addictions. Prior to obtaining my Master Degree in Marriage Family Therapy, I was working in a factory during the decade it was illegal for me to drive. For that reason, I was forced to car pool with two other employees. Every day after work, they had a ritual of stopping at the liquor store to buy themselves a "cold one". They would finally get home and become inebriated every night. Neither had ever been exposed to church in their youth and both had a great deal of baggage from their past and that was their way of dealing with it. They had no support system and life as they had elected to embrace it, was hard.

Or consider Tina, who was abused by her husband at a very early age. She had been forced into submission by her rogue male of a husband. He would at times even publically humiliate her. As if that wasn't enough, he publically had an affair with another woman. Tina was a trained medical assistant and often times had drugs at her discretion. To mask the pains on the home front, Tina turned to substance abuse to mask the pains she had encountered from her husband. As with most addicts, denial was one of the first warning signs of addictive behavior. Tina would take Oxicotton in the evening to throw her into a stooper and she would take Xanax in the mornings; both of which were very addictive.

Tina was removed from her position as medical assistant when the situation came to light. She began to have some major withdraws which caused her to resort to street drugs. With time, Tina finally located a supplier on the street and met monthly with the supplier. People who really knew Tina encouraged Tina to get help, but she would laugh it off, "I'm fine. It's nothing I can't manage." Tina's "management" was a mask to the truth of her being chained to an addictive behavior that dictated her outlook on all of life.

Tina's choices had expensive price tags. The initial marriage reached a point of dissolution following the affair of her husband. She was given custodial care of her daughter. In the court proceedings, Tina had sobered up and masked her addictive history. Once the custodial care of their daughter was finalized, Tina resorted to the drug scene to manage her addictions. She had yet to reach an understanding that she had become a hostage in her chains of addictions. She couldn't really move forward in life. Now that she is sober, she has stated, "In reflection, I was emotionally numb through the whole addictive process. I couldn't feel the pains and joys of life. I simply existed for the next fix."

Tina did re-marry when she had met her new husband on the internet. One thing her new husband was oblivious to was Tina's drug scene and chemical dependence. When questioned by her new husband regarding the medicines she was on, Tina became defensive and would use blame shifting to deflect anyone who questioned her drug use.

Finally it happened. Her new Husband Tim was in panic mode. He came home from a half day at work on Saturday. Tina was in a stooper with the dosage she took. Tim called to see what he should do. I escorted them to a detoxification center where Tina had demonstrated elevated resistance but finally consented. Tina was an in-patient for ten days and was released with a prescription for sub oxen which would cause her to get sick if she resorted to street drugs again.

Tina had become a participant in Narcotics Anonymous. She said NA was resourceful but they were neutral on faith and spirituality. Tina embraced the spiritual dance with her Creator.

God became real to her and she was like a kid in the candy store with her faith and experiences she encountered when she embraced the spiritual dance with God. She could feel again. She was no longer numb to reality. She stopped listening to secular music and resorted to Christian music and radio. She grew in her faith and wanted to be used by God to share her story with others to help prevent youth or troubled teens.

Tina had a history with church and embracing her parents' faith. However, she had never fully experienced her faith until the chains of addictions were broken and the truth had truly set her free. In reflection Tina admitted eight years of her life had been snuffed from her in her relationships with both her daughter and her new found husband; eight years she could never reclaim. I introduced her to Jeremiah 29:11-13 which was God's words to Israel when they were being taken into captivity.

> [11] For I know the plans I have for you," declares the LORD, "plans to prosper you and not to harm you, plans to give you hope and a future. [12] Then you will call upon me and come and pray to me, and I will listen to you. [13] You will seek me and find me when you seek me with all your heart. [14] I will be found by you," declares the LORD, "and will bring you back from captivity. [b] I will gather you from all the nations and places where I have banished you," declares the LORD, "and will bring you back to the place from which I carried you into exile."
>
> Isaiah 40:30-31 says,
>
> [30] Even youths grow tired and weary,
>   and young men stumble and fall;
>
> [31] but those who hope in the LORD
>   will renew their strength.
>   They will soar on wings like eagles;
>   they will run and not grow weary,
>   they will walk and not be faint.

Tina embraced the dance with broken chains that liberated her from the addictive nature she had developed over time. Both Tim and Tina elected to shift from the Karpman Triangle to Chip

Ingrams Godly Triangle and both dedicated their lives to serving God and church. God has used them in a powerful way.

Chemical dependency isn't the only addiction that keeps people in chains. Bill was a confessed Christian. He attended church weekly and went through the motions of worshipping his little god in a box every first day of the week. The rest of the week he kept his god in the box. The Sunday ritual eased Bill's conscience for the rest of the week.

Bill had been placed on night shifts, with no management over him at his worksite on a computer. Every night he would go to porn sites and watch the pornography online. Just like Ted Bundy, Bill acknowledged pornography is progressively addictive. Embracing this as his new normal, it didn't take long before he encouraged co-workers of both genders to watch it with him. Before Bill was caught using company time to watch pornography, he had graduated to oral sex with other coworkers.

When management found out about Bill's use of company time, he was arrested for sexual misconduct. While incarcerated, Bill did some serious soul searching and admitted he had only been a Sunday Christian in his life. He had a belief system, but he admitted he was religiously wrong. Bill had never experienced his faith. Bill said, "Experiencing my faith in an Awesome God is indescribable. It is out of this world. It's as though God has revealed to me the poor choices I was making with my addictions to pornography."

Bill was initially concerned about his marriage and kids following his arrest. After experiencing his faith, God started restoring his relationship between his wife and his children while he was incarcerated.

Bill said he has come to grips that everyone of us has played the prodigal at one point or another. Some of us have more than others but we have all played the prodigal. Bill was released on probation with an early release. His ambitions are to make a ministry for men struggling with sexual sins. He has said he is willing to follow wherever the Lord leads. Bill said, "Prison was what I needed to get my priorities straight and to get in focus once again. Prison has given me living proof that Satan is a liar and a thief always attempting to get people to embrace worldly gain in addictions of every kind. But by the grace of God those chains that held me in bondage have been broken and I have felt free ever since."

Worldly addictions of every kind are a snare of the devil. He persuades us to believe the delusion that is the only way we can manage the pains we encounter throughout life. In retrospect, the only healthy addiction is the addiction presented by Carmen in Concert, "Addicted to Jesus". Jesus wants us to come running to Him with His opened arms. That is how you will become intoxicated with Christ and His purpose in your life.

Some become addicted to soap operas. They live for their soaps. It consumes their conversations with others. It dictates their outlooks on life and after all it is evident, everyone else is doing it. You only live life once. Others are addicted to Facebook in their virtual world of gaming with others they rarely see. Facebook is a recent source of communication and advertising. Many have embraced it so much that it dictates what they have time to do. "I can't leave this game or the virtual foods will spoil". I'll finish it and do my Bible study or devotion tomorrow." Without a healthy self control, Facebook can become quite addictive.

Others are addicted to work and haven't the time of day for spouse and kids, much less God. They eat, breathe and sleep work. They take on work that requires a minimum of 80 hours a week. They are convinced the success of the company is on their shoulders alone. No one can do it as well or as efficient as them. They obsess about the small stuff. They bring home the money but they haven't time to enjoy it. Work is his/her purpose in life. They have withdraws when removed from the work setting due to illness and the like.

Some are addicted to power. This is found a lot in law enforcement and government settings. That's why you hear plastered across the media Politian's involved in extortions and sex scandals. They have stretched limousines five bedroom mansions, a yacht in several ports to retreat to. They have crossed ethical standards and moral lines to get to the top at all costs. In the process, marriages often crumble and families fall apart.

There are some who are addicted to spending or hoarding money. "He who dies with the most toys wins" is the philosophy of many. It's all about the money and the aristocracy that results. "We have to keep up with the Jones'." "Money is the answer to every problem I have." The writer of Hebrews wrote,

"[5]Keep your lives free from **the love** of money and be content with what you have, because God has said,
"Never will I leave you;
never will I forsake you."[a] [6]So we say with confidence,
"The Lord is my helper; I will not be afraid.
What can man do to me?"[b]

Jesus even said in Luke 6:13:

"No servant can serve two masters. Either he will hate the one and love the other, or he will be devoted to the one and despise the other. You cannot serve both God and Money."

Any addiction can ensnare us with obsession which gets us off course from our Maker and lures us into a trap that chains us as hostage to the addiction. To all who have been lured into addictions, be of good cheer. When you are willing to break the chains and you are willing to surrender everything to your Maker, the healing process begins. God will start to work a miracle in your life. So I encourage you to embrace the dance with broken chains, because God longs to dance with you again. The choice is yours. Will you have enough faith to embrace the dance?

1. With the example of Tina, what does the adversary use to lure us away into addictive behavior?

2. As indicated with Tina, life for her had become emotionally painful and difficult. What are some of the painful events of your own life or the lives of others you know, who succumbed to addictions to mask the pains?

3. In reflection, can you recall a coworker or family member or perhaps even your own relationship with a rogue male, who refused to submit to the will of God or any other authority? How did they deal with the pains of the abusive relationship? Why?

4. What is the immediate response of an addicted person when someone questions their addictive behavior? Why?

5. What is the motive of the adversary, when he inspires the addicted to resort to drugs and alcohol?

6. Why did God allow the people of Israel to go into captivity if he truly had great plans for his people?

7. With God's promises to us in Isaiah 40:30-31, why do people resort to addictions instead of running back to The Good Shepherd?

8. What are some other addictive behaviors aside from substance abuse? How do they impact the lives and relationships?

9. Understanding the variety of addictive behaviors our culture has embraced, what addiction has the adversary attempted to ensnare you into? How did you respond to the lure Satan placed before you?

10. What obsessions and compulsions have resulted to the addictions you have encountered?

11. How does God encourage balance regarding the workaholic?

12. What is the only way to truly break the chains of addictions both physically and spiritually?

Embracing the Dance with the Great Commission

In my childhood, I was brought up as a fundamentalist in the Christian Church. Unless you were a Campbell/Stone Believer, based out of the Restoration Movement following the Cane Ridge Revival, in Cane Ridge, KY, you were not considered a brother. What many fail to embrace with that entire belief system was the fact that both Stone and Campbell were Presbyterian. They had from 20,000 to 30,000 people embrace the revival at Cane Ridge and it lasted for weeks. I have longed for another Great Awakening to occur in America once again.

I have even prayed for it as have many others. All Christian walks of faith in Christ to promote unity in fulfilling the Great Commission as we have been called to do. For centuries, Satan has ravaged the church to a point of splitting churches and fracturing their ability to fulfill the Great Commission as we were called to do. God with the unity of His church that has been able to unite for the cause of Christ could retake this great nation of ours. With a third Great Awakening, Christ and His church He has called together, would be unstoppable. Satan knows that so he puts in overtime to keep dissensions in Christ's church over some really petty issues. He has to keep our sights off of the inevitable power of Christ's Church with Him being the head of the church.

My entire childhood, I heard it again and again, Christian churches are actually the only people who are going to make it to Heaven. All others are of the devil. Many said the only Authorized Version was the King James Version that was written in old English in the 1600's. Then discrepancies just didn't add up. You would see God working in the Baptist camp and the Presbyterian camp and the Methodist and Nazarene camps. God started to stir in the hearts of in the Assemblies of God and the apostolic teachings. It just didn't make since. Rather than buying into the enemy's trap of dissension, perhaps it would be better to do as the people of different faiths did when they had the Cane Ridge Revival. Churches refused to bring dissension and promoted unity with grace and God placed the American Communities into faith based communities that kept God at the helm of the American culture. As "One Great Nation Truly under God", God granted us success after success. As a nation under God we were made into a super power internationally.

Satan has ravaged the churches with dissension and traditions that have ensnared and weakened the churches. As a mighty oak, we have allowed ourselves to be splintered into tooth picks that are not healthy enough to reclaim and restore Christ's church as He called us to do, as He was ready to ascend back to His Father's right hand. I have crossed denominational lines to preach the Gospel of Jesus Christ with love and extending a right hand of fellowship to other brothers and sisters.

The apostles did the same thing when they brought Jews and Gentiles to worship together.

Were there differences?

You bet.

Did any of them have unanswered questions?

Absolutely!

Did they share in fellowship together?

Without question. And what was the outcome? They rocked the world with their united efforts toward the cause of Christ's church and people were added to ***the*** church **daily.**

I long for the day when blinders in the church communities are removed and we can truly grasp II Chronicles 7:13-15which says:

[13] "When I shut up the heavens so that there is no rain, or command locusts to devour the land or send a plague among my people, [14] if my people, who are called by my name, **will humble themselves and pray** and **seek my face** and **turn from their wicked ways,** _**then**_ **will I hear from heaven and will forgive their sin and will heal their land**. [15] Now my eyes will be open and my ears attentive to the prayers offered in this place.

Before the Great Commission can be fulfilled, God is calling His Church to unite like never before. Strings by themselves can be crushed and easily broken. But you weave those strings together into a rope and the strength becomes phenomenal. God is calling His Church to unite in strength to prepare for a spiritual battle that is at hand. The line has been drawn between believers verses non-believers. Jesus has called us to prepare for battle.

Listen to the words written by John following Jesus vision to him on the island of Patmos.

[11]I saw heaven standing open and there before me was a white horse, whose rider is called Faithful and True. With justice he judges and makes war. [12]His eyes are like blazing fire, and on his head are many crowns. He has a name written on him that no one knows but he himself. [13]He is dressed in a robe dipped in blood, and his name is the Word of God. [14]The armies of heaven were following him, riding on white horses and dressed in fine linen, white and clean. [15]Out of his mouth comes a sharp sword with which to strike down the nations. "He will rule them with an iron scepter."[a] He treads the winepress of the fury of the wrath of God Almighty. [16]On his robe and on his thigh he has this name written: KING OF KINGS AND LORD OF LORDS.

The efforts in Oklahoma have recently united all denominations to implement the faith initiative. They have been doing some phenomenal things in their efforts and have even encouraged members to live by faith.

I will end this chapter and this book with a few simple mathematical equations. Suppose a congregation of 100 embraced the Great Commission literally. Suppose everyone each committed themselves to saving at least one person per year and add them to the church. In 365 days, our attendance and membership would jump to 200 who share the same commitment. Consider the table below.

Starting of this faith based initiative 100

First Year 200

Second Year

400

Third Year800

Fourth Year

1600

Fifth Year 3200

In five years alone, we will have duplicated 32 times what we started out as. Ministry is not for micromanagement Christians. The Great Commission is far greater than that. In fact it is so great the only way it will ever be completed is if we submit to Jesus Christ and His Word and surrender everything to his calling and follow His leading in this mega outreach effort.

I once travelled with an Amish bishop. I asked him to explain his faith and belief system. There were so many parallels between the Amish and Christian faiths, I went on to ask, "If we worship the same Father, Son and Holy Spirit, what keeps us from sharing in worship and fellowship?" I went on asking, "What prevents your ministers preaching to the English churches and us preaching in your churches?"

His reply was profound. "Because of the hardness of our hearts."

It is time for a heart transplant one at a time to reclaim Christ's church to what He called it to be over 2000 years ago.

Many churches have been critical of one another when all of them have struggled in upholding the biblical premises of church and worship. Many have embraced the critical spirit rather than encouraging dialogue between camps. Jesus criticized the religious leaders of His day. If He issued a report card to our ministers of the gospel today, I wonder what the report cards would look like.

I try to live every day as though it were my last. I have embraced the three tiered circles of influence that was demonstrated by Jesus in His three year ministry efforts.

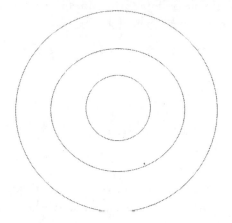

Three Spheres of Influence

Jesus had an inner circle of friends; Peter, James and John. These were the men who knew everything about Jesus. Had there been any sin in Jesus' life, they would have known it. But Jesus was without sin as all three attested. To maintain fellowship, accountability and having someone who has got your back when backed into a corner. The magic number for Jesus was three.

His second sphere of influence was the number of people Jesus could impact and change in the three year ministry tour throughout the regions of Israel. He was able to equip twelve to change the world and pass the Paton to in the ministry effort, which is exactly why small groups of twelve are encouraged in growing churches.

The outer sphere is your circle of impact. Through the people you cross paths with regularly; people you work with or people you go to class with or civic groups you participate with. The number in this sphere can range from one hundred to limitlessness.

If you ultimately want to "Embrace the Dance with an Intimate God", you must also "Embrace the Dance with the Great Commission." God has made the invitation to dance with you and to totally turn this world upside down. Only you can determine if you are willing to Embrace the Dances of Life with Him or not. Go ahead! Take that step of faith and see how God wants to use you to serve His purpose in life. Come on, ... Embrace the Dance!

1. With the example of Tina, what does the adversary use to lure us away into addictive behavior?

2. As indicated with Tina, life for her had become emotionally painful and difficult. What are some of the painful events of your own life or the lives of others you know, who succumbed to addictions to mask the pains?

3. In reflection, can you recall a coworker or family member or perhaps even your own relationship with a rogue male, who refused to submit to the will of God or any other authority? How did they deal with the pains of the abusive relationship? Why?

4. What is the immediate response of an addicted person when someone questions their addictive behavior? Why?

5. What is the motive of the adversary, when he inspires the addicted to resort to drugs and alcohol?

6. Why did God allow the people of Israel to go into captivity if he truly had great plans for his people?

7. With God's promises to us in Isaiah 40:30-31, why do people resort to addictions instead of running back to The Good Shepherd?

8. What are some other addictive behaviors aside from substance abuse? How do they impact the lives and relationships?

9. Understanding the variety of addictive behaviors our culture has embraced, what addiction has the adversary attempted to ensnare you into? How did you respond to the lure Satan placed before you?

10. What obsessions and compulsions have resulted to the addictions you have encountered?

11. How does God encourage balance regarding the workaholic?

12. What is the only way to truly break the chains of addictions both physically and spiritually?

Biography

John W. Gasser graduated from Johnson Bible College in 1985 with a Bachelors Degree Preaching Ministry. In 2002, John returned to JBC to pursue his Masters Degree in Marriage Family Therapy. He achieved this goal in 2004.

John has been a Counselor for six years and a Minister of the Gospel for 20 years. God has called him to churches ranging from the Mountains of North Carolina to the country fields of Indiana. His counseling ministry has taken him from private practice to counseling in the prisons and everything in between.

John married his best friend, Laura Thomas in 1981. She has blessed him with three beautiful children, Tabitha, John Thomas, and Benjamin. Their family has expounded to five grandchildren and one on the way.

John enjoys camping, boating and helping those in need. John felt compelled by the Holy Spirit to compose this book and prays that this will help readers embrace the dances of life with anticipation, to help them maneuver around every challenge life dishes out. John hopes and prays this writing will be used for God's Purpose and glory for impacting the lives of others.